W9-AEU-855

PEAK PERFORMANCE
Coaching the Canine Athlete®

M. Christine Zink DVM, PhD

Canine Sports Productions
12701 Folly Quarter Rd.
Ellicott City, MD 21042
443-535-9145
www.caninesports.com

Copyright © 1997 by M. Christine Zink

Illustrations © 1992 by Marcia R. Schlehr

All rights reserved. No part of this publication may be reproduced or transmitted in any form or by any means, electronically or mechanically, including photocopying, recording, or by any information storage or retrieval system — except by a reviewer who may quote brief passages in a review to be printed in a newspaper or magazine — without written permission from the publisher.

Coaching the Canine Athlete is a registered trademark.

Published by: **Canine Sports Productions**
            12701 Folly Quarter Rd.
            Ellicott City, MD 21042

ISBN 1-888119-02-0

First Printing 1997, Second Printing 2000, Third Printing 2004

Limits of Liability and Disclaimer of Warranty:

The author and publisher shall not be liable in the event of incidental or consequential damages in connection with, or arising out of the furnishing, performance, or use of the instructions or suggestions contained in this book.

Books are available at special discounts for bulk purchases for sales promotions, fund raising, or educational use. For details contact:

Canine Sports Productions
12701 Folly Quarter Rd.
Ellicott City, MD 21042
Phone 443-535-9145
Fax 443-535-9146
www.caninesports.com

Printed in the United States of America

To all of those
whose invitations to me
have included the words,
"And bring the dogs."

Peak performance happens when peak preparation governs the effort.

CONTENTS

Deborah Lee Miller-Riley/Animals Only

THE AUTHOR

A dog-lover all of her life, Chris Zink got her first dog, an Irish Wolf-hound, the day she graduated from the Ontario Veterinary College with her DVM. From an initial interest in obedience, mainly as a survival tactic, she gradually became fascinated with all aspects of canine performance. She currently shares her home with three Golden Retrievers and two Maine Coon cats. Dr. Zink has put over 45 titles in obedience, agility, retrieving, and conformation on dogs of several different breeds from the Sporting, Working, and Hound groups.

While competing in performance events throughout Canada and the United States, Chris recognized a significant information gap. Owners and trainers wanted to know more about how canine structure and medical or physical conditions affect their dogs' performance, and how to keep their canine teammates healthy and injury-free. Yet little information was available. She therefore wrote *Peak Performance: Coaching the Canine Athlete*, a comprehensive guide to the dog as an athlete. Her second book, *Jumping From A to Z:*

Teach Your Dog to Soar, coauthored with Julie Daniels, has become the gold standard for jump training.

Dr. Zink presents Coaching the Canine Athlete® seminars worldwide and regularly writes articles for dog magazines. She is also a consultant on canine sports medicine, evaluating canine structure and locomotion, and designing individualized conditioning programs for active dogs.

In her other life, Chris is a veterinary pathologist and an Associate Professor at Johns Hopkins University School of Medicine, with over 70 scientific publications. There, she teaches Pathology to medical and veterinary students and does AIDS research.

ACKNOWLEDGMENTS

Although there is only one author listed on the cover of this book, many people contributed to it, both directly and indirectly. I am indebted to Marcia Schlehr, Janet Gauntt, Janet Lewis, Ruth Barrish, Linden Craig, Dee Dee Rose, Sally Josselyn, Phyllis Autotte, Amy Meyer, and George W. McCulloch for reading the original manuscript and providing many valuable suggestions borne out of their widely varying experiences and expertise. I thank my careful editors of the Second Edition: Debbie Spence, Jane Jackson, Terri Clingerman, Liby Messler, and Dee Geisert who combed the manuscript for typos and errors and gave me much encouragement. Marcia Schlehr provided the thoughtful and accurate illustrations, made possible by decades of the study of canine structure. I would also like to acknowledge the input from many unnamed friends who have generously offered snippets of information, many of which have become part of my knowledge base. I thank Doug Windsor, Marcia Halliday, and Leigh Palmer for providing me with my Golden friends and teammates. Finally, I am grateful to Marcia Halliday, Cynthia Fox, Julie Daniels, and Dawn Hayman for teaching me to look past the obvious in my quest to understand dogs.

The radiographs for this book were provided through the courtesy of Dr. Paul Pennock and the Ontario Veterinary College, Guelph, Ontario, Canada. The radiographs were photographed by Tim Sullivan, and prints were made by Pathology Photography at the Johns Hopkins Medical Institutions.

INTRODUCTION

To a man the greatest blessing is individual liberty;
to a dog it is the last word in despair.
William Lyon Phelps

People obtain dogs for a variety of reasons. Most often, people choose a dog because they want it to share in their lives. An avid runner may want company on those three-mile runs in the early morning. Another person wants a couch companion for evening television. A third loves to go backpacking in a nearby wilderness area and knows that a dog is the perfect, quiet companion.

A growing segment of the population enjoys pursuing dog-related activities for exercise and the fun of competition. Competitive dog sports began in the late 19th century as hunting competitions and soon expanded to include conformation shows. Today, in addition to field trials and conformation shows, organized dog sports include events such as obedience, agility, tracking, herding and hunting tests, lure coursing, Schutzhund, sledding, carting, flyball, water rescue, draft dog tests, terrier trials, and many more!

There are many books that discuss the specifics of how to train dogs for particular performance events. But training is only one facet of preparing for competition. The dog must be physically prepared in a broader sense, starting with a sound body strengthened through exercise, proper nutrition, and excellent health care. We, as owners/trainers/handlers, participate in canine performance events by playing the role of coach. The winning coach must be a combination of talent scout, sports medicine specialist, problem preventer, physical therapist, trainer, and friend.

This book is written for people who wish to coach their dogs to peak performance, whether for the private pleasure of a weekend hike or for organized canine sports events, and who therefore want to learn more about the dog as an athlete. It explains the structure of the canine body and how each part of the body functions. It provides detailed information on how to keep your dog physically fit and mentally ready for action. It also details the many genetic defects, medical problems, and medications that can adversely affect canine performance.

Every pastoral society has developed herding dogs. The structure of each breed reflects its original function.

1.

HOW STRUCTURE

AFFECTS FUNCTION

The dog is man's best friend.
He has a tail on one end.
Up in front he has teeth
And four legs underneath.
Ogden Nash

THE IMPORTANCE OF STRUCTURE

Observe the athletes competing in track and field events at the Olympics. Famous marathon runners such as Bill Rodgers and Frank Shorter are of moderate height, have a small frame, and are very lean and wiry. In contrast, short distance runners and hurdlers like Carl Lewis and Edwin Moses are often taller, more muscular, and larger-boned. These physical differences are partly genetic and partly due to conditioning. A smaller and, thus, lighter person is likely to have an advantage over a heavier person in long-distance running where endurance is a key factor. In contrast, height, or at least long legs, is a definite advantage for a hurdler.

Each year, hundreds of young girls between six and eight years of age apply for entry to a selective ballet school in New York City. Before the children are interviewed or auditioned, their bodies are measured. The length of each girl's spine, neck, leg and arm bones, and feet are recorded and entered into a computer. A program is then run which provides information as to whether the child's body structure has the potential to mature into one that is ideal for ballet.

Given a suitable structural framework, proper conditioning is still necessary to take advantage of that genetic potential and to achieve peak athletic performance. Thus, marathon runners use a training program that emphasizes the strengthening of certain muscle groups more than others, while a training program for hurdlers will strengthen a different complement of muscles. Similarly, girls with appropriate body types are accepted into ballet school, and training that capitalizes on their current structure begins. The conditioning and skill training maximize their potential.

Careful, focused training can overcome some deficiencies in genetically determined structure, permitting the athlete to excel in spite of a less-than-ideal body type. Most basketball players, for example, are genetically tall. However, there are several excellent players who, although much shorter than their teammates, excel because of their coordination, timing, and physical strength.

The relationship between structure and function is just as important in dogs as it is in humans, especially in dogs that are expected to perform athletically. The success of a dog in performance events is dependent both on its genetically determined structure and on its physical fitness achieved through conditioning and training.

In the wild, all carnivores are performance animals. Wolves and other related canids have specific body types because they need to hunt to survive, and natural selection favors only those individuals whose structure enables them to be fast enough and strong enough to capture their prey (Fig. 1.1). Those individuals born with genetic defects detrimental to performance are less likely to survive, and their defective traits are eliminated from the gene pool.

Wild carnivores were domesticated thousands of years ago. Whether humans domesticated the dog or the dog first attached itself to humans is open to debate. In any case, a relationship between man and canine began to develop, with each party benefiting from the interaction. Dogs were provided with food and shelter. Humans, in turn, capitalized on the dog's physical strength, instincts, and intelligence for a variety of tasks. By selective breeding, mankind molded the dog into a variety of shapes and sizes to suit different functions.

Large dogs, resembling today's Mastiffs, were used in warfare and as guard dogs. These were heavyset dogs whose massive heads and powerful jaws proved a good deterrent to robbers. Large, fleet-footed dogs such as the Irish Wolfhound were used by hunters to capture and kill animals for food.

Medium-sized dogs resembling today's pointers, setters, and spaniels were used to find game for the hunter. The game was netted by the hunter or

Fig. 1.1. A coyote's physique enables it to trot long distances at moderate speeds in the pursuit of game. It is light-boned to reduce body weight and has moderate angulation of the limbs to give it speed and agility when hunting.

killed by falcon or arrow. Later, after the development of firearms, retrievers were developed; their job was to fetch the birds killed by the hunter. Dogs that bore a resemblance to predators such as wild dogs or coyotes were used to herd sheep. The sheep had a natural fear of these dogs and would run away when they came too close. This is the basis of herding. These dogs did the work of several shepherds, enabling a single person to tend many more sheep.

Smaller dogs also served in many capacities. Those with short legs, known as turnspits, were used to help with the cooking. They were placed in a wheel at one end of a roasting spit where they walked, much like a hamster in an exercise wheel, thus rotating the meat roasting above the fire. In 17th century England, dogs were kept in churches to warm the feet of churchgoers. Dogminders were hired to keep the dogs under control during the church service. (Apparently this had limited success, because it is recorded that in 1636, the Bishop of Norwich was forced to have rails and pillars built to keep the dogs away from the Communion bread!)

Few dogs were kept solely as pets, and these were owned almost exclusively by the very affluent, such as kings, emperors, and other nobility. The Pekingese is one example — a dog selectively bred for its lion-like appearance, which appealed to the Chinese emperors who kept them as lap dogs.

From these beginnings, humans took advantage of the plasticity of the dog's genetic makeup, its short gestation period, and its large litter size to further mold the dog into an amazing variety of shapes and sizes in a relatively short time span. Nowhere else in the animal kingdom do we find animals of the same genus and species that are so different in appearance. Surprisingly, the Irish Wolfhound is more closely related to the Chihuahua than the gray fox is to the red fox.

The most extreme changes in the physical appearance of dogs have been made during the 20th century with the advent of dog shows. Lithographs depicting dogs in the 18th and 19th centuries show many recognizable sporting breeds, hounds, and terriers, but with less extreme features than those of their modern counterparts. Today, the features of many breeds are more exaggerated: Collies have longer muzzles, Bulldogs have more flattened faces, English Setters have more profuse feathering, and Bloodhounds are more wrinkled.

The breed standards, which are written descriptions of the appearance of a perfect (though nonexistent) member of each breed, provide guidelines that detail the physical appearance considered ideal for the breed. Most breed standards emphasize the relationship between the dog's appearance and the original purpose of the breed. For example, terriers were used to hunt vermin, and had to crawl into holes in the ground to capture their prey. Thus, the Border Terrier was bred to have a bold, feisty temperament, a very strong, compact body, and a tough, wiry coat which was resistant to damage and protected the skin.

Scenthounds, because of their superior sense of smell, were used in hunting. The Basset Hound's distinctive body type evolved so that these dogs would be close to the ground where the scent is more abundant, and slow enough to be followed on foot. They were also bred to have long, pendulous ears to waft scent toward the nose.

Sporting dogs, such as the Chesapeake Bay Retriever, were bred to hunt waterfowl and upland game birds, such as pheasant and quail, at short distances. Thus, these animals were bred to stand alongside the hunter, to have a strong retrieving instinct, and to be able to run and swim while carrying a bird. Fully

Table 1.1 Performance Events	
Event	*Breeds*
Conformation	Any purebred dog
Obedience	Any purebred or mixed breed dog
Tracking	Any purebred dog
Agility	Any purebred or mixed breed dog
Flyball	Any purebred or mixed breed dog
Field Trials, Hunting Tests	Sporting breeds (retrievers, setters, pointers, spaniels) and hunting hounds (Beagles, Basset Hounds and Dachshunds)
Coonhound Events	Black and Tan Coonhounds, Bluetick Hounds, English Hounds, Redbone Hounds, Plott Hounds, Treeing Walker Hounds
Herding Trials & Tests	Herding breeds, some Working breeds
Lure Coursing	Sighthounds
Terrier Trials & Earthdog Tests	Smaller terriers and Dachshunds
Schutzhund	Any purebred or mixed breed dog that can perform the required exercises
Sledding	Any purebred or mixed breed dog
Draft Dog Tests	Bernese Mountain Dogs, Saint Bernards, Bouvier des Flandres, Rottweilers, Newfoundlands
Weight Pulling Competitions	Any dog, whether purebred or mixed breed
Water Rescue	Newfoundlands, Portuguese Water Dogs

25 percent of the breed standard of the Chesapeake Bay Retriever describes the dog's distinctive double coat which protects the dog as it retrieves waterfowl in the cold weather conditions of the region for which it was named.

Toy breeds, such as the Maltese, were bred to be lap dogs. They were developed strictly for the pleasure of their company. Thus, the Maltese has a long, pure white coat which requires a great deal of grooming. The Maltese's coat and perky little face with dark eyes and nose make it resemble a stuffed animal.

Performance events began as a forum for owners and handlers to show off their dogs' talents. Initially, dog shows took the form of hunting/retrieving competitions, and these were soon followed by herding trials. Gradually these early performance events were expanded to include exhibitions in which dogs were benched (stationed in a particular spot) for examination by both the judges and the public. The last 15 years have seen an increase in the number and variety of performance events available to dogs and dog-lovers. Table 1.1 gives a partial list of today's canine performance events and the breeds that participate in them.

The best-attended performance events today are conformation shows. Their primary purpose is to give breeders an opportunity to have their dogs evaluated and compared with the theoretical ideal dog of that breed (the breed standard) by an impartial authority. Dogs shown in conformation must be in peak physical condition in order to best approximate that ideal. There is no breed standard which states that the ideal dog of that breed should be "flabby, moderately overweight, and with a pendulous abdomen." Instead, many standards expressly state that the dog should be physically fit. For example, the Labrador Retriever standard states that dogs of that breed should be "strong and muscular." Thus, conformation shows are a type of performance event, open to dogs of all breeds, for which the dogs should be in peak condition.

Many other performance events, such as obedience, tracking, and agility, are open to dogs recognized by the organizations which set forth their own rules and regulations. In some competitions, although dogs of particular breeds may excel, other dogs are welcome to participate. (A team of Standard Poodles has done a credible job of running the Iditarod, a 1,158-mile sled dog race in Alaska.) Other events are open only to specific breeds. For example, only the Sporting breeds and some Hounds may participate in American Kennel Club field trials.

Canine performance events can be highly competitive, especially at the upper levels, and dogs participating in these events may be required to perform complex physical maneuvers with a great deal of accuracy. For example, in obedience competitions, a dog is required to perform the same exercises whether it weighs 10 or 100 pounds. Because of differences in body type, some breeds have advantages or handicaps in certain exercises. It is much easier for a Brittany than for a Mastiff to jump an obstacle its own height at the withers

Fig. 1.2. Brittany easily clearing a jump one and a quarter times its height at the shoulder.

Fig. 1.3. Mastiff jumping an obstacle its height at the shoulder.

(Figs. 1.2, 1.3). A larger dog, on the other hand, may have an advantage in scaling a 6-foot high agility A-frame. This obstacle must seem like a skyscraper to the toy breeds. Thus, it is easier for dogs of certain body types to excel in certain types of performance events, although other dogs, with proper training and conditioning, can also perform well.

Regardless of body type, dogs that participate in performance events experience a variety of physical and emotional stresses that may make them subject to degenerative problems or injuries. Therefore, a thorough knowledge of how structure affects function and how function, in turn, affects structure, is essential for success in performance events and for keeping the canine half of the team healthy and injury-free.

Participation in canine performance events requires that the handler/ trainer have all of the attributes of a coach of a winning track and field athlete. He or she must:

1. Have knowledge of structure as it is related to movement.
2. Institute proper conditioning techniques for the dog relative to both its genetic structure and the task(s) required of it.
3. Be able to detect signs of injury and illness.
4. Provide or obtain proper therapy and veterinary care when necessary.

CANINE FUNCTIONAL ANATOMY

The dog's body is a marvelous package, with each part having a specific role to play in performance. A knowledge of canine anatomy is an essential first step in understanding how the different parts of the dog's body function in performance and in designing an appropriate conditioning program. In the following pages, the various parts of the canine body are described in relationship to their functions (Figs. 1.4, 1.5).

The Relationship Between Body Type and Performance

There are three broad classifications of body type in people (although individuals may combine characteristics of more than one type), and these classifications can be applied to dogs.

Ectomorphic (*ecto* = outside, *morph* = shape) people are tall, generally slender people with long legs and arms. These individuals excel at sports that require endurance, such as marathon running. The correlate in dogs would include most of the sighthounds — breeds such as the Saluki, the Greyhound, and the Scottish Deerhound — and other long-legged breeds such as the Weimaraner. Ectomorphic dogs have an advantage in jumping events due to their longer legs and higher center of gravity.

Mesomorphic (*meso* = middle) people are of medium size, have strong bones, and are well-muscled. Extrapolating to dogs, the mesomorphic body type would include such breeds as the Labrador Retriever, the Beagle, the Portuguese

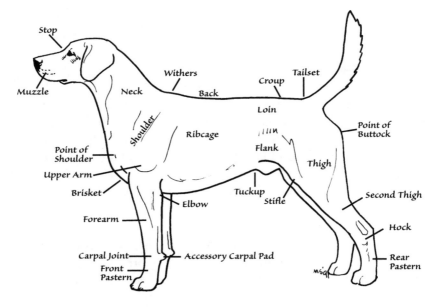

Fig. 1.4. External anatomy of the dog.

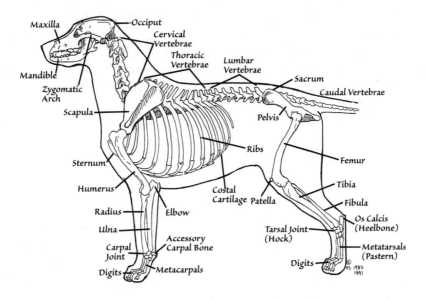

Fig. 1.5. Side view of a dog, illustrating the names and locations of various bones. (From: Marcia R. Schlehr, *A Study of the Golden Retriever*, Travis House, Clinton, MI, 1982.)

Water Dog, the Keeshond, the Border Terrier, and the Australian Cattle Dog. The moderate body type of a mesomorphic dog is suitable for competition in a variety of performance events.

Endomorphic (*endo* = within) people are generally of normal height, but have a tendency to be more heavyset or overweight. They build muscle more easily than ectomorphic individuals and excel at sports that require strength, such as football and weight lifting. Dogs of endomorphic body type include the Bernese Mountain Dog, the Bullmastiff, the Bulldog, and the Clumber Spaniel. These dogs carry more weight on their frames and therefore have to work harder at movements, such as jumping, that require them to move rapidly or turn quickly.

The spectrum of body types seen in performance events is broadened even more in dogs, because certain breeds have been bred for gigantism or dwarfism. Within the giant breeds, there are dogs of ectomorphic body type such as the Irish Wolfhound, of more mesomorphic body type, such as the Great Dane, and of endomorphic type, such as the St. Bernard and Newfoundland.

The numerous dogs that have been bred for dwarfism come in two types: chondrodysplastic dwarfs and pituitary dwarfs. Chondrodysplastic dogs have shortened legs but relatively normal-sized bodies and heads. Examples of such breeds include the Basset Hound, the Corgis, the Dachshund, the Pekingese, and the Dandie Dinmont Terrier. These breeds are really charming but have special needs with respect to performance events. For example, the short front legs and relatively long body put them at a disadvantage in events requiring jumping. Other breeds have been selectively bred to be very small but with a normal relationship between body length and leg length; these are the pituitary dwarfs. Toy breeds with this appearance include the Toy Poodle, the Chihuahua, the Papillon, the Maltese, and the Miniature Pinscher.

The Head

> So the heart be right, it is no matter which way the
> head lies.
>
> Sir Walter Raleigh

There are three types of heads in dogs: dolichocephalic (*dolicho* = long, *cephalic* = head), mesocephalic (*meso* = middle), and brachycephalic (*brachy* = short). Dolichocephalic heads are elongate and narrow, through both the muzzle and the back skull (Fig. 1.6). Breeds with dolichocephalic heads include the Collie, the Whippet, and the Borzoi. This shape of head can be associated with

Fig. 1.6. A Collie has a dolichocephalic head.

Fig. 1.7. A Chesapeake Bay Retriever has a mesocephalic head.

Fig. 1.8. A Pug has a brachycephalic head.

certain genetic problems (described later). Mesocephalic heads are moderate in
proportion, with the length of the muzzle nearly the same as the length of the
back skull. The back skull is generally broader in width than the muzzle
(Fig. 1.7). Breeds with mesocephalic skulls include the Labrador Retriever, the
Dalmatian, and the Norwegian Elkhound. Dogs with brachycephalic skulls have
shortened faces. In these dogs, the width of the skull is at least 80 percent of its
length. These dogs frequently have wrinkled skin over the muzzle and face,
somewhat protruding eyes, and an undershot jaw (Fig. 1.8). Breeds of dogs with
brachycephalic heads include the Bulldog, the Pug, and the Pekingese. Dogs
with brachycephalic heads may be handicapped in some performance events,
particularly those that require long distance running and physical endurance,
because they may have abnormalities in the internal structure of the nose and
upper respiratory tract. Despite these problems, dogs with brachycephalic skulls
appeal to many people, perhaps because their flattened faces look somewhat
human.

The Nose

> *My nose is huge! Vile snub-nose, flat-*
> *nosed ass, flathead, let me inform you*
> *that I am proud of such an appendage.*
> Cyrano de Bergerac

A dog's nostrils are comma-shaped to encourage scents to swirl around
inside the nasal passages. The nose has voluntary muscles that flare the nostrils
to pick up more scent. Inhaled odor particles are dissolved in the mucus layer of
the nose, and then transported to the cells below. These cells receive information about the amount and type of scent and transmit this information to the
brain. There are millions of these cells in multiple, scrolled chambers within the
dog's nose. Tests have shown that dogs are capable of discriminating a single
molecule of one scent in the midst of three trillion others.

Man has learned to capitalize on dogs' superior sense of smell in a
variety of ways. Dogs are used at airports to detect drugs and other types of
contraband. Dogs guard monuments and buildings and sniff visitors in order to
detect explosives. Search and rescue dogs are used to locate lost people and
victims of natural disasters such as earthquakes. A number of performance
events are designed to test dogs' sense of smell. Tracking tests, Schutzhund
competitions, retrieving tests, and Utility level obedience all require that dogs
discriminate among objects with different odors.

The Whiskers

Not by the hair of my chinny chin chin.
The Three Little Pigs

Whiskers are modified hairs that give dogs an amplified sense of touch. Dogs have whiskers scattered around their muzzles, over their eyes, on the sides of their cheeks, and underneath their chins. The whiskers are thick, specialized hairs that sit anchored under the skin within a small pool of blood surrounded by many nerve endings. When the hair is moved, waves are created in the pool of blood. This stimulates the nerve endings, sending messages to the dog's brain.

In cats, the whiskers are used as a guide to the size of space through which the cat can fit. It is unlikely that this is true in dogs, since most dogs are much wider than their whiskers. Nonetheless, the whiskers are an additional means by which the dog gathers information about its environment; in this case, by the sense of touch. For example, when the whiskers around the eye are touched, a reflex causes the eyes to shut, thus helping the dog to avoid objects that may injure the eye. The whiskers are important for dogs working in heavy vegetation and may be critical for search and rescue dogs and avalanche dogs that work in areas with uncertain footing. Some people also believe that slight alterations in whisker position are used in canine communication.

We do not know whether whiskers aid dogs in performance activities such as tracking or the obedience scent discrimination exercise. Although few (if any) breed standards insist that the whiskers be cut, this practice is common in many breeds shown in conformation.

The Mouth

"My what big teeth you have," said Little Red Riding Hood.
"All the better to eat you with, my dear," said the Wolf.
Little Red Riding Hood

Most breeds of dogs are required to have 42 teeth (Fig. 1.9). There are six incisor teeth, both top and bottom, across the front of the mouth. The function of the incisors is to nip and pull at objects. Next to each outside incisor is a long canine tooth used for gripping and shredding and to prevent carried objects from being dropped. Behind each canine tooth on the upper jaw are four premolar teeth and two molar teeth. On the lower jaw there are four premolars and three molars. The premolars and molars are used for shearing and grinding. On each side of the mouth, top and bottom, there is a very large molar tooth with

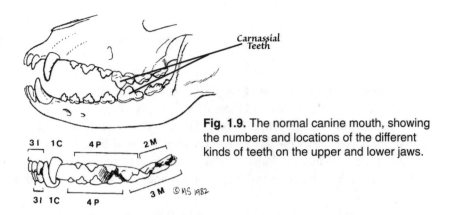

Fig. 1.9. The normal canine mouth, showing the numbers and locations of the different kinds of teeth on the upper and lower jaws.

many points, called the carnassial tooth. These are the teeth that your dog uses to tear holes in your brand new leather shoes.

Each dog has two sets of teeth during its lifetime. Puppies are born without teeth, but generally by two weeks of age their small, deciduous teeth have begun to appear. Between the ages of two and six months, the deciduous teeth are pushed out by the erupting adult teeth. The smaller the breed of dog, the later the eruption of the permanent teeth.

Most breed standards describe the ideal bite for that breed. Most of the Sporting and Working dogs are expected to have a scissors bite, with the upper incisors overlapping the lower incisors so that the inner surface of the upper incisors contacts the outer surface of the lower incisors (Fig. 1.10). Other breed standards, particularly those of some Herding breeds, require or accept a level bite. In a level bite, the incisors meet without overlapping (Fig. 1.11). Many brachycephalic breed standards specify that the ideal dog should have an undershot jaw with corresponding bite. This means that the lower incisors project forward beyond the upper incisors (Fig. 1.12).

Often, the ideal bite for a breed reflects a particular function of that breed. For example, a level bite may help a herding dog to nip at the heels or the flanks of the animals it is herding. Sometimes, however, a breed standard lists a particular bite as acceptable simply because that is the most common bite found in that breed. This is the case in many of the breeds with brachycephalic skulls. In these breeds, it can be difficult to retain the desired appearance of the head without an undershot jaw. Thus, this bite may be accepted as normal for these breeds. Conditions of the teeth that can affect performance are discussed in Chapter 7.

Fig. 1.10. Scissors bite. (From: Schlehr, *Golden Retriever.*)

Fig. 1.11. Level bite. (From: Schlehr, *Golden Retriever.*)

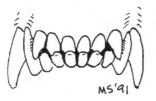

Fig. 1.12. Undershot jaw. (From: Schlehr, *Golden Retriever.*)

Dogs competing in performance events are required to use their mouths in a variety of ways. Dogs being shown in conformation must, of course, approximate as closely as possible the tooth structure required by the breed standard. Because dogs that compete in field trials and hunting tests are required to carry game birds in their mouths, most of the Sporting breeds have what is termed a "soft mouth;" they do not exert much pressure on the object they are carrying. A wooden obedience dumbbell will last years when used with a soft-mouthed dog. Other dogs, particularly the Working and Herding breeds, grip objects much more tightly in their mouths. Dogs used in Schutzhund activities are required to grip a canvas sleeve and tug at it very hard without letting go. These dogs need to have strong teeth and jaws, and it is not desirable for them to have a soft mouth.

The Eyes

Jeepers Creepers - where'd you get them peepers?
Johnny Mercer

Canine eyes are similar in shape to those of humans, except that most of the white (sclera) is hidden by the eyelids. Dogs may have blue eyes or any shade of brown eyes, from almost yellow to very dark brown (or one of each color). In most breeds, the eyelids are supposed to fit snugly to the eyeball. If the eyelids are too tight, or if the eye is very deep set, the eyelids will roll inward (entropion) and cause the eyelashes to irritate the cornea. If they are too loose, the eyelids droop outward (ectropion), collecting grass seeds and dirt that can damage the cornea and irritate the tissues of the eyelid.

Although the visual acuity of dogs is not tested in routine ophthalmological examinations, studies have shown that the acuity of dogs' vision is similar to that of humans. However, dogs are better at detecting motion and have a much wider visual field and better night vision than humans.

In the past, dogs were thought to be color blind, but more recent studies have shown that this is not the case. At the back of the eyes (in the retina), there are structures called cones that detect color. There are three kinds of cones in the retina of the human eye: they detect blue, green, or red light. Working together, they detect all of the colors we recognize. Dogs, however, lack the cones that detect the color green. The colors green, yellow, orange, and red all appear as yellow to the dog, whereas blue and purple look just the same to a dog as they do to us. This impaired color vision (red-green color blindness) is used to advantage in training dogs for field trials or hunting tests. Fluorescent orange retrieving dummies (which, like the grass, appear yellow to the dog) are used as "blinds;" objects that the dog cannot distinguish visually and must be located by taking direction from the handler.

The Ears

It's all very well to be able to write books,
but can you waggle your ears?
J. M. Barrie to H. G. Wells

The ears have three parts: the outer, middle, and inner ears. The outer ear consists of the ear flap and the ear canal leading to the ear drum. Dogs' outer ears may be erect, folded in various ways, or dropped (Figs. 1.13 to 1.15). Dropped ears are common in many Sporting and Working dogs that have been bred for swimming, and may help prevent water from getting in the ears. Some think that dogs with erect ears have better hearing, but this is difficult to prove because it is difficult to test for small differences in the acuity of dogs' hearing. In North America, some breeds, such as the Doberman Pinscher, the Boxer, and the Schnauzers, have cropped ears. These dogs would have dropped or semierect ears if left unaltered. In most cases, puppies of these breeds have their ears cosmetically altered by surgery at approximately three months of age to make them stand erect. Breeds such as the Irish Terrier and the Pug are bred to have folded ears simply to give a pleasant appearance to the head. A dog's ears are very mobile; most dogs can turn their ears 180 degrees. Thus, the dog can rotate its ears to face the direction from which a sound originates or to change its facial expression as a part of communication. In a dog showing dominance, the ears are pricked up and pointing forward. A dog demonstrating submission will lay its ears flat against its neck. There are many other ear positions which dogs use to express happiness, playfulness, curiosity, lust, and a variety of other emotions.

Selective breeding for function has affected ear shape, too. Dogs who were bred for the now-outlawed sport of fighting have small ears which were less susceptible to damage. Hence, the Bulldog, which a century ago was used for bull-baiting, has small ears that can be laid back flat against the head. Other breeds, particularly those used for scent work, were bred to have large, pendulous ears which are thought to aid the dog in picking up scent.

The middle ear consists of the eardrum and several small bones that pick up vibrations from the eardrum and stimulate nerves in the inner ear that send messages to the brain. Dogs have much more sensitive hearing than man. Dogs can hear sounds at wavelengths up to 50,000 cycles per second (Hz), whereas man has an upper range of 20,000 Hz.

The ear also functions in balance. The balance mechanism of the inner ear consists of three semicircular canals oriented at right angles to each other. These canals are filled with fluid that moves with changes in position and sends messages via nerves to the brain as to which end of the dog is up. Chronic ear

Fig. 1.13. A Cardigan Welsh Corgi has erect ears.

Fig. 1.14. A Shetland Sheepdog has folded (semi-prick) ears.

Fig. 1.15. A Flat-Coated Retriever has dropped ears.

infections can damage the inner ear, causing loss of balance or loss of coordination. This sometimes manifests itself outwardly as a tilted carriage of the head.

The Coat

And Joseph had a coat of many colors.
The Old Testament

Dogs' coats have probably been changed more by selective breeding than any other single physical characteristic. The canine genome has many genes for coat color that are easily reassorted and recombined. Dogs come in hundreds of different colors and color combinations.

Dogs can be either double-coated or single-coated. Examples of double-coated breeds include the Golden Retriever, the Shetland Sheepdog, and the German Shepherd Dog. A double coat is made up of an outer coat of coarse guard hairs and an undercoat of densely-packed finer hairs. There is a ratio of approximately one guard hair to ten undercoat hairs. Air becomes trapped within the dense coat and its natural oiliness creates water-resistance. Dogs with double coats can swim in cold water or work in the rain and still maintain their body temperature. In addition, one shake removes most of the water from the skin surface. Most double coats are of medium length, and all double-coated breeds shed their hair. Whether the dog sheds seasonally or throughout the year depends on the individual and its environment (both temperature and day length).

In dogs with single coats, all of the hairs are of equal thickness and texture. Single coats may be of any length, from the long, flowing coats of the Lhasa Apso and the Yorkshire Terrier to the short coats of the Dalmatian and the Pharaoh Hound. Some of the single-coated breeds, such as the Poodle and the Kerry Blue Terrier, do not shed but have coats that must be trimmed regularly.

Coats serve a variety of functions in dogs. Sporting dogs have been bred for coats that can withstand the climate in which they are expected to perform: a wide range of temperatures, rainy weather, fresh and salt water, snow, and thick ground cover. For these dogs, it is important that the coat protect the skin without being an encumbrance. Within individual Sporting breeds, there often are differences in coat characteristics between dogs bred for field work and those bred for the show ring. Thus, English Setters bred for field trials have shorter, somewhat wavy coats, while English Setters shown in conformation have much longer, straighter coats.

Dogs with medium to long coats have an advantage in top-level obedience trials, a sport in which a dog that is a mere one or two inches out of position is penalized. Small infractions of this nature are much harder for a judge to detect on a medium- or long-coated dog than on a dog with a very short coat, such as a Greyhound or a Doberman Pinscher.

For some dogs, coat color is related to function. The Nova Scotia Duck Tolling Retriever (a Canadian Sporting dog) is a small, red dog with white on the tip of the nose, the top of the head, the tip of the tail, and the feet. These dogs play with each other by the side of a pond and attract the attention of ducks overhead, which fly in to investigate the moving red and white objects. This activity is called tolling. The ducks are then shot by hunters, and the dog completes its duties by retrieving the ducks.

Another example of functional coat color and texture can be seen in the Komondor, a large dog with a long, white, corded coat. When the animal is young, the coat is soft and curly. As the puppy grows, the hairs of the coat clump together and form elongate mats called cords. When these dogs are full grown, their abundant, corded coat makes them resemble sheep, at least at a distance. The function of the Komondor is to guard sheep against predators. To do this, they mingle amongst the sheep, in essence becoming a member of the flock — a dog in sheep's clothing. The heavy, matted coat also serves as protection against the environment and as armor when fighting predators.

Some of the original reasons for breeding dogs of specific colors have been lost, and one can only speculate as to why such a variety of unique coat colors were developed. Does the typical Border Collie have white points on a black background so that it can be readily seen by the shepherd a long distance away on the Scottish hills? Certainly the coat color of many breeds today is related more to whim or fancy than anything else. What else would account for the coloring of the Dalmatian or the Harlequin Great Dane? Coat color can be associated with debilitating, even fatal diseases in dogs. Some of these conditions are discussed in Chapter 7.

The Back

The backbone's connected to the hipbone.
Children's Song

The dog's spine consists of a series of bones — the vertebrae — that surround the spinal cord. The spinal cord transmits messages regarding voluntary movement from the brain to the limbs. The spinal cord is also the control

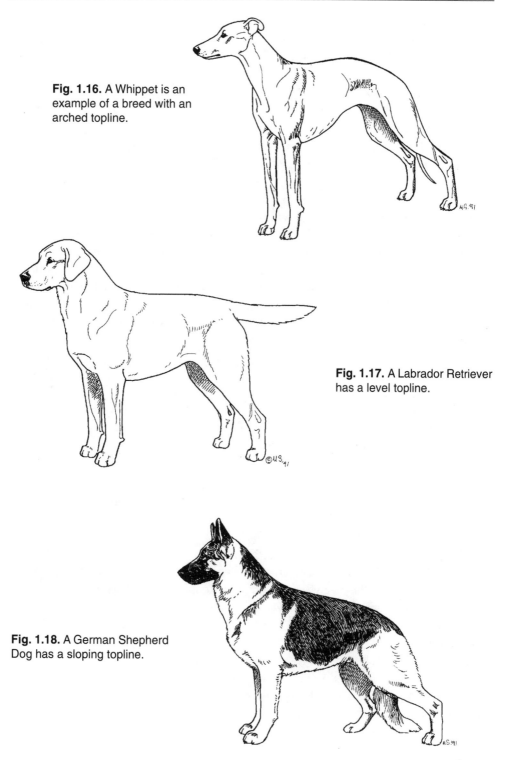

Fig. 1.16. A Whippet is an example of a breed with an arched topline.

Fig. 1.17. A Labrador Retriever has a level topline.

Fig. 1.18. A German Shepherd Dog has a sloping topline.

center for reflexes (automatic movements made without conscious thought). The vertebral bones are wrapped in many crisscrossing muscles and are connected to each other by joints and ligaments.

The top of the dog's profile from the shoulders to the base of the tail is referred to as the topline. The topline may be arched over the loin, as is seen in the Scottish Deerhound and the Whippet (Fig. 1.16), it may be level, as in the Skye Terrier and the Labrador Retriever (Fig. 1.17), or it may be sloped, as in the German Shepherd Dog (Fig. 1.18).

The topline of a dog is associated with that breed's primary working gait. The toplines of many of the dogs which were bred for running at a gallop are arched. This enables greater flexibility and permits these dogs to tuck their rear legs well up underneath their bodies, thus increasing the amount of ground covered with each stride. Dogs with level toplines are comfortable galloping for short distances or cantering but often use the trot as their main distance-covering gait. Dogs that have sloping toplines often have noticeably more angulation of the rear legs than the front, resulting in a lowered rear and, thereby, a sloping topline.

It is critical that the dog's spine be strong enough to support the midsection of the body with its vital organs, yet flexible enough to permit smooth gait and agility. A weak, sagging topline can be a genetic conformational fault, or it may result from a lack of fitness; dogs that are physically fit have well-developed muscles over their neck, shoulders, loin, and hindquarters.

The Tail

> *This is a case of the tail wagging the dog.*
> Anonymous

Dogs' tails come in many lengths, from the long, plumelike tail of the Borzoi to the small, bobbed tail of the Rottweiler. Dogs with bobbed tails may be born that way, or they may have their tails docked a few days after birth. Breed standards generally give very specific details as to the correct length of the tail, and an incorrectly docked tail can be an impediment to a dog's conformation show career.

The tail helps the dog maintain its balance, especially when jumping, turning at fast speeds, accelerating, and braking. In jumping, the dog's tail is held low as it takes off, and as the dog nears the top of its arc, the tail flicks upward. This shifts the animal's center of gravity forward, raising the rear and helping to propel it over the jump. As the dog lands, the tail falls back downward, aiding in balance. Dogs with bobbed tails can jump well, but use a different jumping style to accommodate for the lack of a tail counterweight.

The tail is also used as a rudder during swimming. When a dog swims, the tail is held straight out just under the surface of the water. When the dog turns, the tail swings to the side, pushing against the water and helping the dog to turn. The heavy tail of a retriever may also help balance the weight of game carried in its mouth.

The tail is used in communication, both with other dogs and with humans. A wagging tail may express contentment and is a dog's equivalent of smiles and laughter. In other contexts, a stiffly wagging tail which swishes back and forth deliberately can be a form of threat. Like the ears, a tail held high can indicate confidence or aggression, and a tail held low and tucked between the legs may be a sign of submission or anxiety.

The Chest

He may have hair upon his chest
But, sister, so has Lassie.
Cole Porter

The chest contains the heart and lungs, two organs that are so vital that they are completely surrounded and protected by the bones of the ribcage. There are variations among breeds in the relative length, width, and depth of the chest. Regardless of breed, the chest must be large enough to permit maximal expansion of the lungs. Many of the fastest running breeds, such as the Greyhound, have very deep, narrow chests. This allows expansion of the lungs without increasing wind resistance. This narrowness also contributes to efficient action of the legs alongside the thorax or forechest. The deep chest tends to limit these dogs at rest because they are not as comfortable lying on their chests or in a curled position as they are when lying on their sides. Breeds for which speed is not so critical tend to have a somewhat wider ribcage. At the other extreme is the Bulldog. Bred for stability on the ground, this breed has a chest that is as wide as it is deep.

The heart, vascular system, and lungs function together to provide the body with oxygen. Of all the organs in the body, skeletal muscle utilizes the most oxygen. Thus, adequate heart and lung function are critical in performance. The heart is the center of the cardiovascular system, a network of branching blood vessels that course through every millimeter of the body to

provide oxygen and nutrients necessary for life. The heart is basically a muscular pump. Its function is to pump blood to the lungs to be oxygenated, then to
send the oxygenated blood and nutrients to the rest of the body, since oxygen is
necessary for all cells to function. The heart is very complex, and when the
puppy is developing as a fetus, the heart undergoes many changes in shape. This
increases the likelihood of developmental defects, and defects of the heart are
among the most common congenital abnormalities in puppies. Some of these
congenital defects are not compatible with life, while others delay development
and maturation. Other problems may not be detected until the dog is grown and
it becomes evident that the dog lacks stamina. Common defects of the heart are
discussed in Chapter 7.

The red blood cells, the most numerous of the cells in the blood, contain
hemoglobin. This molecule is designed to carry oxygen from the lungs through
the vascular system and release it into the tissues. The red blood cells are
shaped so that they can squeeze through the smallest spaces to carry oxygen to
every part of the body. Each time the heart beats, these cells are pumped from
the heart to the lungs, where they travel through many tiny capillaries adjacent to
the air sacs of the lungs. There, they exchange oxygen for carbon dioxide.
When they return to the heart, they are pumped with great force through the
arterial system and into the tissues of the body. After releasing oxygen into the
tissues, they make their way back into the venous system and return to the heart
to be recirculated. The blood pressure is much higher in the arterial portion of
the cardiovascular system than the venous portion, and if an artery is injured, a
great deal of blood can be lost in a short period of time.

The major function of the respiratory system is to extract oxygen from
inhaled air (which consists of only 20 percent oxygen) and transfer it into the
cardiovascular system. The contraction of the diaphragm and expansion of the
ribcage cause the lungs to expand and air to be drawn in through the nose, past
the larynx (where the vocal cords are), down the trachea, or windpipe, and
finally through multiple branching airways, and into the air sacs (alveoli) within
the deepest lung tissue. The alveoli have thin walls which permit the exchange
of oxygen and carbon dioxide molecules. Once this exchange has occurred, the
diaphragm pushes the deoxygenated air out of the lungs.

Another function of the respiratory system is vocalization. Animals such
as fish and some amphibians that breathe through gills are unable to vocalize,
but animals with a larynx are able to deliberately make sounds. Barking in dogs
is produced by the forceful expulsion of air out of the lungs and past the vocal
cords in the larynx. The vocal cords vibrate, producing the noise with which dog

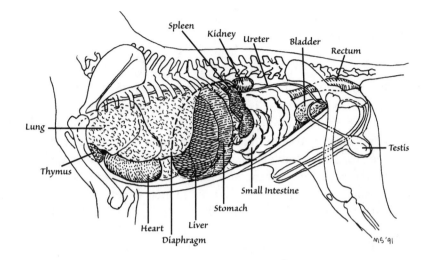

Fig. 1.19. Internal organs of the chest and abdomen.

owners are so familiar. By contracting the muscles that surround the larynx and by adjusting the strength and timing of the contraction of the diaphragmatic muscles, the dog can growl, howl, yip, yodel, and make many other interesting and occasionally aggravating sounds.

The Abdomen

> *He had a broad face and a round little belly*
> *that shook when he laughed like a bowl full of jelly.*
> Clement C. Moore, "A Visit From St. Nicholas"

The abdomen is basically a large sac that contains the organs of a number of body systems including the digestive system, the urinary system, the reproductive system, and parts of the endocrine system (Fig. 1.19). The abdominal cavity is surrounded by three sets of muscles which protect the abdominal organs and assist in movement.

The Digestive System

The organs of the digestive, or gastrointestinal, system are predominantly involved with taking in food, processing it for the body's use, and eliminating waste. Adequate functioning of the digestive tract is critical in the performance dog, who needs to make maximum and efficient use of its available food. The parts of the gastrointestinal system include the mouth, the esophagus, the stomach, the small and large intestines, and the rectum and anus. This, of course, is the path that food takes through the body. There are also a number of glandular organs — the salivary glands, the pancreas, the liver, and the gall bladder — that participate in the process of digestion and absorption of food.

The mouth takes food into the body, chews it, and swallows it. Moisture is added to the food by the salivary glands. The food then passes down the esophagus and into the stomach. The stomach contains acid and digestive enzymes that are mixed with the ingested food again and again by the contractions of the stomach. Between the stomach and the intestines there is a circular muscle called the pyloric sphincter which permits the contents of the stomach to enter the small intestines a little at a time. Once the material enters the small intestine, digestive enzymes are added from the pancreas. The pancreas secretes three types of enzymes: amylase to degrade carbohydrates, trypsin to digest proteins, and lipase to break down fat. Bile acids from the gall bladder, which help to break up fats, are also added to the contents of the small intestine. The main function of the large intestine is to remove water from the intestinal contents and return it to the body so that the animal does not lose too much fluid in the digestive process. The stool then passes out of the dog's body.

Nutrients from the gastrointestinal tract pass through the liver before entering the blood to be distributed throughout the body. The liver checks the nutrients for toxins and attempts to degrade them if they are present. It also metabolizes fats, carbohydrates, and proteins, storing some of them and turning others into forms that are more readily utilized by the body.

The Urinary System
The main function of the urinary system is to remove waste products from the blood. These waste products, which are continually produced by every cell in the body, enter the blood and are brought to the kidneys. Each kidney has a complex physical and biochemical mechanism that filters blood and removes waste products while retaining the blood cells and nutrients that are necessary to the animal. The waste products, in the form of urine, then enter the bladder where they are stored temporarily and released periodically.

The Reproductive System
Dysfunctions of the male and female reproductive systems, particularly hormonal imbalances, can cause significant problems in performance dogs. The male reproductive system consists of the testes and epididymis, which sit in the scrotum (actually an outpouching of the abdominal cavity), the vas deferens, which transports sperm from the testes to the penis, the prostate gland, which secretes fluid to help the sperm to survive longer outside of the body, and the

penis. The female reproductive system includes the ovaries, oviduct, uterus, vagina, and mammary glands. The ovary is the site where eggs (ova) mature and are deposited at regular intervals into the oviduct to be transported to the uterus. If fertilized, the eggs will stay in the uterus which then nurtures the embryos as they grow into fetuses and in about 63 days are whelped as puppies. The mammary glands supply nutrients to the puppies in the form of milk. The activities of both the male and female reproductive systems are coordinated by hormones secreted from a variety of endocrine organs throughout the body.

The Endocrine System

The pituitary gland, thyroid glands, parathyroid glands, adrenal glands, pancreas, ovaries, and testes are all considered part of the endocrine system. These glands secrete hormones, biochemical messengers from one kind of tissue that travel in the blood to other tissues with instructions on how they should function. The endocrine system centers around a master organ, the pituitary gland, located at the base of the brain. It secretes many different regulatory hormones that direct hormone production by other endocrine organs. For example, the pituitary gland secretes a hormone which tells the thyroid gland how much thyroid hormone to produce. It also directs hormone production by the reproductive organs, the adrenal gland, and the pancreas. In addition, the pituitary secretes its own hormones which act directly on tissues; an example is somatotropic hormone, which regulates growth. Dogs that are deficient in growth hormone may be only one third the size of their littermates as adults (pituitary dwarfism). Other pituitary secretions are prolactin, which causes the mammary glands to secrete milk, and melatonin, which regulates the formation of skin pigment.

There are two thyroid glands located in the neck just below the larynx. Thyroid hormone regulates the body's metabolic rate and affects the speed at which the cells function. An excess of thyroid hormone will cause the cells to utilize more nutrients, causing weight loss and premature aging. A deficiency of thyroid hormone causes weight gain, hair loss, and a variety of other clinical signs (described in Chapter 7).

The parathyroid glands are two small glands located alongside each thyroid. Their function is to regulate the balance of calcium and phosphorus in the body, and thus they are important for bone growth.

The adrenal glands, located just above each of the kidneys, secrete several hormones. These include aldosterone which regulates thirst, and the sex hormones, estrogen and testosterone, which regulate development of the reproductive organs and reproductive activity. They also secrete corticosteroids, the so-called stress hormones which have far-reaching effects on virtually every tissue in the body. Corticosteroids metabolize carbohydrates, fats, and protein, and help the animal cope with illness and injury. When prescribed inappropriately, they can also impair wound healing and tissue repair and increase susceptibility to infection.

The pancreas, in addition to helping digest food, secretes insulin, a hormone that helps cells absorb sugar from the blood. Since sugar is the main source of energy for cells, a deficiency of insulin (diabetes mellitus) affects the function of every cell in the body

The Autonomic Nervous System

The functions of most of the body systems within the abdomen are modified through nervous impulses delivered by the autonomic nervous system. They are not under voluntary control. The nerves of the autonomic nervous system receive messages from the brain via the spinal cord. The impulses then travel throughout the abdominal cavity to the abdominal organs. The nerves of the autonomic nervous system are of two types: sympathetic and parasympathetic. These two types of nerves have opposite effects on the organs they serve.

The sympathetic nervous system is often referred to as the "fright, fight, or flight" system. When these nerves are stimulated, usually in response to something that is perceived as a possible danger, adrenalin is secreted by the adrenal gland. Adrenalin causes the animal's body to shut down functions that are not critical for immediate survival, such as digestion, and to step up functions that can help the animal to handle the dangerous stimulus, such as mental awareness, cardiovascular function, and muscular activity. Activity of the sympathetic nervous system is the reason that most of us do not feel like eating right before a canine performance event. It is also the reason that people in danger can perform activities that require more strength than they would be capable of under ordinary circumstances.

The parasympathetic nervous system regulates the body's function under normal conditions, when the animal has a feeling of overall well-being. It induces the digestive system to function, permits reproductive activity, slows the heart rate and allows blood to be distributed to the skin and the digestive and reproductive organs. The parasympathetic nervous system tells a dog's bladder to hold urine while it fills and to empty when the bladder becomes full. When puppies reach about four and a half months of age, the voluntary nervous system has developed enough that the puppy is able to consciously overrule this action of the parasympathetic nervous system and hold the urine until a convenient time. This voluntary control is what house training is all about.

The Legs

Dogs, like horses are quadrupeds. That is to say, they have four rupeds, one at each corner, on which they walk.
Frank Muir

The front legs are made up of three main long bones which are analogous to those of the human arm (Fig. 1.20). The scapula, or shoulder blade, lies against the rib cage and is attached to the body not by joints, but by large, fan-shaped muscles. Below the scapula is the humerus, or upper arm, which is joined to the scapula by a ball-and-socket joint, the shoulder joint. The humerus is connected to the two bones of the lower arm, the radius and the ulna, at the elbow. The radius and ulna end at a very complex joint composed of many small bones, called the carpal joint, which is analagous to the human wrist. From the carpal joint, the five metacarpal bones together form the pastern, which ends at the foot.

The rear legs are joined to the body at the pelvis, a large, H-shaped bone attached to the spine (Fig. 1.21). The uppermost bone of the rear leg is the femur. The largest bone in the dog's body, it connects to the pelvis by a ball-and-socket joint, the hip joint. The femur joins with the two bones of the lower leg, the tibia and fibula, at the knee joint (stifle). The knee is a complex joint that is subject to many traumatic and degenerative conditions. The tibia and fibula end at the tarsal joint, or hock, which is analogous to the human heel. Below the hock joint extend the five metatarsal bones, which then join with the bones of the toes.

The bones of the legs form a solid support, a type of scaffolding, on which all of the other body components are laid. The two main functions of the bones are to bear weight and to provide a location for the attachment of muscles. Muscles are always attached at each end to different bones. Muscles work only by pulling (contraction), and this brings the bones closer together. Paired muscles with opposing effects contract alternately, resulting in movement. For the legs to function correctly, the bones must meet each other at proper angles. These angles help to reduce the concussion associated with weight-bearing, and they improve the leverage of the muscles. There is a range of angles over which each joint functions best. The angulation of the joints is one of the factors evaluated by judges in conformation shows. The muscles and the bones always

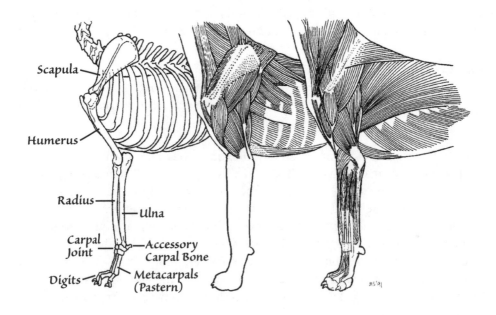

Fig. 1.20. The bones and muscles of the front leg.

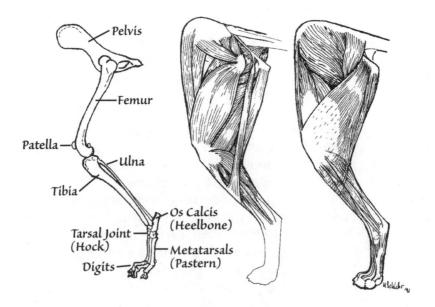

Fig. 1.21. The bones and muscles of the rear leg.

work together and thus are often referred to as the musculoskeletal system. One can view the musculoskeletal system as a crane, in which the bones are the pieces of metal scaffolding that make up the arm of the crane, and the muscles, tendons, and ligaments are the complex system of metal cables, pulleys, and winches that run alongside of the crane arm and do the work.

Running alongside and within the muscles of the limbs are many nerves. The nerves, like electrical wiring, transmit information from the brain regarding the type of movement that is required. In that sense, the brain is analogous to the operator who sits in the cab of the crane and who pushes the pedals and the levers to direct the crane arm and its system of pulleys.

Blood vessels provide oxygen and nutrients to all parts of the limbs so they have energy to operate. This is analogous to the diesel fuel which provides the energy for the crane's work.

Proper functioning of the limbs is critical to performance in dogs. The legs are subject to many degenerative and traumatic conditions, partly because they bear the body's weight, and partly because the legs contain many complex moving parts. In addition, the joints are the target of many genetic problems, including hip dysplasia, elbow dysplasia, and patellar luxation (dislocation of the patella or kneecap), which can have adverse effects on performance. These are described in Chapter 6.

The Feet

> *This little piggy went to market*
> *This little piggy stayed home*
> *This little piggy had roast beef*
> *This little piggy had none . . .*
> Nursery rhyme

Dogs have four weight-bearing toes on each foot. These toes are like the fingers of the human hand. Many dogs also have a vestigial thumb on the inner side of the foot between the pads and the pastern called the dewclaw. Dewclaws are normally present on the front legs at birth. Some breeds have rear dewclaws, as well. The Great Pyrenees and the Briard are required by their breed standards to have double dewclaws on the rear legs. Some breed standards specify whether the dewclaws may be removed. Removal of the dewclaws prevents them from getting caught and injured when dogs are running over rough terrain or on crusted snow. It is relatively easy to surgically remove the dewclaws in puppies at about three to five days of age. Nevertheless, the dewclaws probably

Fig. 1.22. This dog is bearing its weight on the front leg, and the carpus is hyperextended, with the pastern resting on the ground. At this point, the dew-claws may assist in turning by digging into the ground as the dog's leg rotates.

do assist the dog in turning, especially when the dog is bearing its weight on one front leg (Fig. 1.22). At that point, in even the lightest dogs, the pastern is flat on the ground, and the carpal pad cushions the carpal joint as it hits the ground. The dewclaw is in contact with the ground and may assist in turning by digging into the ground as the dog's leg rotates.

There are five pads on the bottom of the dog's foot — one under each toe and one at the center of the foot. The skin of the pads is the thickest skin on the dog's body. The pads provide protection against sharp objects and function as shock absorbers. Along with the claws, they also provide traction. The pads are thickest at the point where they join the claws; this helps the dog to dig its claws in when it needs traction on slippery surfaces.

There is an additional pad at the back of the front leg behind the carpal joint called the accessory carpal pad. As a dog lands after a jump, its pastern overextends slightly, and the pad behind the leg forms a bumper or cushion as it hits the ground (Fig. 1.23). This pad may also be used as a braking device during fast running and turning.

This chapter has outlined only the simplest details of the dog's anatomy. As your dog's coach and trainer, it is important to be cognizant of these details so that you can understand your dog's individual structural strengths and weaknesses and thus help your dog to achieve its greatest potential.

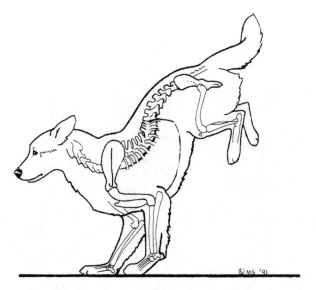

Fig. 1.23. When the dog lands from a jump, the accessory carpal pad on the back of the carpus helps to cushion the landing.

A Mastiff demonstratng a smooth, effortless trot in the conformation ring.

2.

STRUCTURE

AND LOCOMOTION

A dog is not 'almost human' and I know of no greater insult to the
canine race than to describe it as such. The dog can do many things
which man cannot do, never could do and never will do.
John Holmes

INTRODUCTION

Locomotion is the unifying factor in all performance events. In some events, such as conformation and tracking, the dog must perform fairly simple acts of locomotion like trotting or cantering at moderate speeds with few turns. In others, such as obedience and agility, the dog is required to expand its loco-motive capabilities to types of movement that would be well outside of its repertoire were it still in the wild. In obedience trials, a dog must jump rela-tively high vertical jumps. They must also clear a long, flat (broad) jump and turn quickly after landing. The dog's locomotive abilities are further taxed in agility trials in which a dog may be expected to scramble over an A-frame six feet high, and in search and rescue work where a dog may be required to scale a 6-foot solid wall or climb a ladder. All of these acts of locomotion require both a sound, healthy body, and specialized training.

Every newborn puppy, when it first begins to move, starts to send mes-sages regarding movement along specific neural pathways in the brain. These neural pathways are called engrams. They are like ruts in the brain along which the messages prefer to travel. The engrams for patterns of gait are established at a very young age. If, for some reason, a young dog is taught (or allowed) to move in an abnormal or inefficient way, although the dog may be physically capable of moving correctly, the abnormal movement will become habitual because engrams for the abnormal movement have formed. For example, a dog that lives its early life entirely on slippery flooring may habitually move as if it is walking on ice. Only with proper and persistent training can new engrams be forged in the brain, sending signals along the correct pathways, leading to a correct and efficient style of movement.

A dog's movement generally reflects its structure, which is one reason why movement is evaluated in the conformation ring. Structural inadequacies can often be disguised when a dog is shown standing (stacked) or by expert grooming but many of these structural inadequacies will be revealed when a dog moves. Correct physique and physical fitness are essential for proper movement, no matter what the dog's conformation.

Movement involves a series of complex interactions entailing coordinated activity by several body systems. The major body systems involved in movement are the nervous system, the cardiovascular system, and the musculoskeletal systems.

The nervous system has both sensory and motor components. The sensory part of the nervous system sends information regarding the dog's environment and the location of the dog's limbs to the brain. As part of the sensory component, there are many small structures in the skin, connective tissue, and muscle called receptors. There are several types of receptors, each with the ability to sense something different. For example, receptors in the muscles sense when they are stretched. The receptors send messages up the nerves, through the spinal cord, and to the brain. In the brain, the messages are decoded, and the animal becomes conscious of the sensation.

Motor nerves relay signals for the muscles to contract and move each part of the body. The motor component of the nervous system is connected to the sensory component because the animal has to know where its limbs are (through sense) before it can use the motor system in movement. Most of the motor nerves begin in the brain and run down the spinal cord. From there, they go to either the right or the left side of the body where they branch many times like a tree, with each branch providing messages to a different muscle or part of a muscle.

The sensory and motor parts of the nervous system work together in voluntary movement, in which the dog decides where to place its feet, and in reflex movement, in which the motions are automatic and subconscious. Voluntary movement starts as a thought in the cerebral cortex of the brain. This thought is present in the form of electrical impulses that can travel along many different pathways through the brain. The conscious decision to move starts an electrical impulse that proceeds down the spinal cord to the limbs involved in that particular movement. Reflexes, on the other hand, begin in a limb, run up to the spinal cord, and then travel back down another limb.

For example, when the right leg is lifted, a reflex automatically tells the left leg to step down towards the ground. This reflex prevents a dog from falling over if one leg is knocked out from under it. This reflex is also what makes walking and trotting such an automatic process. The dog doesn't have to think about each step it is going to make. It only thinks about moving, and much of the actual foot placement is taken care of by reflexes. There are many other reflexes, such as the one that causes a dog to swing its head toward a painful stimulus, such as a fly bite or a veterinarian's needle, and the one that makes the dog stretch its limbs out as it is being lowered to the ground.

The muscular system consists of both muscles and tendons, the structures that attach muscles to bone. The muscle cells are shaped like long cylinders, and thousands of muscle cells lie side by side in a bundle. Inside each muscle cell, there are two proteins, actin and myosin, which form long, stiff rods. Each actin rod has a myosin rod on either side of it. When the nerve tells the muscle to contract, an enzyme causes the actin and the myosin molecules to slide past each other, thus shortening the muscle. This process takes a great deal of energy, and muscle tissue is one of the greatest utilizers of energy in the body. Each dog is born with a certain number of muscle cells. As a dog becomes more fit, each muscle cell becomes larger by accumulating more actin and myosin.

The tendons are made of very tough connective tissue. They have great tensile strength but have a limited ability to stretch, and thus can be damaged when excessive tension is put on them. Attached to each tendon are stretch receptors which send messages to the brain that tell just how much contraction of the muscles has taken place.

Bones are made up of connective tissue with minerals added for hardness. Although it would seem that a tissue as solid as bone would be static in shape and size, bones are actually changing all of the time in response to stresses put on them. Thus, the bones of heavyset dogs tend to be more dense than those of lighter dogs, because their bones have responded to the greater weight. If a dog carries its weight on the outside of a limb, the bones will eventually change shape so that they can better bear weight in that area.

The bones meet each other at the joints, which are surrounded and held together by a tough tissue called the joint capsule. In addition, the bones are joined to each other and supported by ligaments, bands of parallel fibers that are similar in composition to tendons. (Tendons join muscle to bone, whereas ligaments join bone to bone.) Ligaments are made up of microscopic parallel fibers that are folded like an accordion within a sheath. When the ligament is pulled, the fibers straighten out within the sheath. However, if the ligament is overstretched, the fibers will break, resulting in partial or complete tear of the ligament. Ligaments have very little regenerative capacity, and when torn, they heal by laying down scar tissue, a stiff tissue with minimal ability to stretch. Thus, ligaments that are torn do not return to full function after healing because they heal by scarring. The joints contain synovial fluid, a slippery substance that reduces the friction of the bones rubbing against one another just as oil reduces wear on the pistons in an engine.

To provide leverage, many bones are joined at angles. The degree of the angles between the bones of the front or rear legs is referred to as angulation. If a dog has too little angulation, the movements of the leg will not be as powerful because the muscles do not have sufficient leverage. In addition, the dog will suffer increased concussion each time the foot bears weight because there will be less flexibility in the limb as it lands. This increases the chances of the dog developing degenerative joint disease (discussed in Chapter 6). On the other hand, if a dog has excessive angulation, the limbs will be less stable. Excessive angulation may predispose the dog to ligament damage because the ligaments may be subjected to more stress than they can withstand.

GAITS

Surprisingly, every dog, regardless of its shape or size or its proportion of body length to height, follows the same general pattern of movement and has a similar repertoire of gaits. The main types of canine gait are the trot, the canter, the gallop, and the walk. In the trot, diagonal limbs move forward at the same time. That is, the dog's right front leg and left rear leg move forward together followed by the left front leg and the right rear leg, which also move together (Fig. 2.1). In the trot, diagonal pairs of legs bear weight alternately so that there are two moments of weight bearing. A trotting dog should have a fluid movement with little vertical or lateral motion. All of the dog's energy should be expended in moving the body forward. The front foot should extend forward to a point below the dog's nose. This forward swing of the leg is referred to as reach. Dogs with a short upper arm and/or poor angulation of the forelimb often have shorter reach. When trotting, the dog's rear legs should move freely and

Fig. 2.1. Side view of a dog trotting, Diagonal legs move forward together.

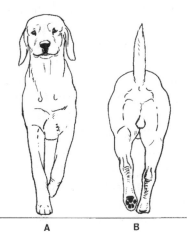

Fig. 2.2. A toy Poodle trotting, demonstrating reach and rearward extension (drive). Note how the handler has dressed to complement her dog!

Fig. 2.3. Front (A) and rear (B) views of a dog trotting, showing proper conformation of legs and single tracking.

A   B

straighten almost completely as they stretch out behind. This is referred to as rearward extension or drive (Fig. 2.2). Good reach and rearward extension will increase a dog's length of stride. A dog with good reach and rearward extension will expend less energy while covering the same amount of ground as a dog that must take many shorter steps.

Ideally, dogs moving at a moderate trot should tend to single track. This means that, as each foot falls, it lands under the midline of the dog's body (Fig. 2.3). If the dog were to trot through snow, one could observe that the paw prints left behind form a relatively straight line. As the dog increases in speed, the feet should move closer to the center line. Single tracking allows the dog to maintain its center of gravity over the support point (foot) so that it doesn't have to shift its weight from side to side as would be the case if the footfall were wide of the center line. When a dog has to shift its weight from side to side, it wastes energy and there is greater stress on the bones and ligaments.

An observer, looking at a dog moving toward him, should see that the front legs form a straight line from the shoulder to the foot. The dog's elbows should not bend inward or outward, nor should the pasterns (Fig. 2.3A). The dog should not throw its elbows out, nor should it flip its feet out before they land. When a dog is viewed moving away from the observer, the rear legs should present a similar picture in which the legs from the hip to the foot form a straight line, not bending outward or inward at the stifle or the hock (Fig. 2.3B).

In conformation shows, gait is evaluated by observing the dog working at a moderate trot. There are several reasons for this. One reason is that the trot is a symmetrical gait. The dog's legs are paired in their pattern of movement, unlike in the canter or the gallop. This makes the movement much easier to assess. In addition, the trot is slow enough to be observed easily by the trained human eye. Finally, the trot is a natural gait for most dogs. For wild dogs, the trot is the preferred mode of locomotion at a moderate speed.

There is, however, a problem with assessing all dogs at a trot — the trot is not the preferred performance gait for all dogs. For example, the Greyhound would be best evaluated at a gallop — the gait it uses on the race track or while chasing a lure. The Mastiff is probably best evaluated at a walk, the gait it uses most when guarding its master's property. Dogs have structural modifications that improve their performance at their ideal working gait, and these may be incompatible with the idealized trot. For example, the rear legs of Border Collies are often cowhocked (hocks turned inward). This structure helps them to lie down and get up quickly and to make sharp turns in response to the movements of sheep. A cowhocked dog does not have the ideal appearance at the trot, because the legs are not straight when viewed from the rear. Although the Border Collie standard allows these dogs to be slightly cowhocked, judges who are less familiar with the Border Collie standard will not look favorably upon cowhocked dogs, and they will be penalized. The result may be that Border Collies bred with conformation competition as the primary goal will have straight rear legs and may not function as well in sheep herding, their original function.

A second canine gait is the canter. In the canter, the rear legs land almost at the same time, with one leg just ahead of the other. The leg that lands in front of the other (i.e., the one that hits the ground second) is called the lead leg. The front lead leg bears the entire weight of the dog while the rear legs are swinging forward and thus is usually the dog's stronger leg. (Just like us, dogs are right- or left-sided; right-sided dogs most frequently use the right front leg as lead and vice versa.) For example, in a dog that is leading with the left front leg, one rear leg lands first, followed by the opposite rear leg and the right front leg landing simultaneously. Next, the left front leg lands, and it bears all of the dog's weight while the other three legs are gathered under the dog to prepare for the next stride (Fig. 2.4). In the canter, there are three weight-bearing moments — it is a three beat gait.

The gallop is the fastest of the canine gaits. There are four moments of weight-bearing in the gallop — one rear leg lands followed by the other rear leg, then one front leg lands followed by the other (Fig. 2.5). The head and neck assembly play a significant role in the balance of the cantering and galloping dog. As the dog gallops, it thrusts its head forward and down, shifting the body's center of gravity forward, much as a runner pumps the arms. When the rear legs have moved underneath the body, the head is drawn up and back, and the center of gravity shifts toward the rear of the dog. As the dog gathers its legs underneath, then reaches forward for another stride, the spinal cord flexes and extends (Fig. 2.6). Thus, a well-muscled head and neck assembly that moves freely from the shoulders, and a flexible spine can greatly increase the efficiency of the canter and the gallop.

During the walk, each leg alternately reaches forward, first one front leg, then the diagonal rear leg, then the other front leg and the other rear leg (Fig. 2.7). This happens in rapid succession and weight is generally borne on three of the limbs at any given time. Thus, the walk is a four beat gait.

Fig. 2.4. The canter.

Fig. 2.5. The gallop.

Fig. 2.6. In the gallop, a dog's spine undergoes extreme flexion.

Fig. 2.7. Side view of a dog walking. Three of the dog's legs are bearing weight.

Fig. 2.8. Side view of a dog pacing. The legs on the same side move together.

A   B

Fig. 2.9. Two examples of the same breed: one (A) with straight shoulders and the other (B) with proper shoulder angulation.

The trot is the most commonly seen two beat gait. Another is the pace.
Unlike the diagonal trot, the pace is a lateral gait during which the dog's front
and rear legs on the same side move forward together (Fig. 2.8). Dogs are often
unwittingly trained to pace rather than trot by their handlers. As a dog quickens
its walking speed, legs on the same side of the body naturally begin to move
forward together. This fast walk is called an amble, a gait that is often mistaken
for pacing. In the amble, as in the walk, three feet are on the ground at any
given time. If the ambling dog moves faster, he can easily begin pacing since his
front and rear legs are already swinging forward almost at the same time. Shifting from a pace to a trot requires that the dog first take a stutter step with the
rear legs so that the diagonal legs begin to swing forward together. If a dog is
first trained to move at a fast walk (amble), and then its speed is gradually
increased, the dog may become a habitual pacer. This often happens with a
trainer's first serious obedience dog, because the trainer moves slowly while
learning the footwork, then gradually speeds up as she becomes more proficient.
Dogs cannot move as smoothly nor turn as efficiently when pacing because the
center of gravity keeps shifting from side to side. Thus, a pacing obedience dog
frequently lags since it cannot accommodate to the required speed changes. In
obedience, pacing dogs most commonly lag on the outside loop of the figure 8,
after U-turns, and when asked to accelerate from slow to normal or from normal
to fast speeds.

To move smoothly and efficiently, a dog needs the correct amount of
front and rear limb angulation for its preferred gait. Figure 2.9 shows two dogs
of the same breed with different shoulder angulation. The more the angulation,
the greater the stride (step) length (Fig. 2.10). But, more important than the
angulation of either the front or rear legs is that the dog have balanced angulation of the front and rear. This is particularly important when the dog is trotting,
since the opposite front and rear legs must work together. In the most common
kind of imbalance, the front legs are less angulated than the rear. The reduced
reach of the front legs means they will take less time to swing forward than the
rear legs. To coordinate the landing of the diagonal front and rear legs, the dog
must hold the front leg in the air while the rear leg finishes its forward swing.
As a result, the dog may flip the front feet at the end of the forward swing, raise
the front legs in a hackney gait, or swing the front legs to the side as they swing
forward. Lack of balance is the origin of many common front leg gait abnormalities.

Interference is another consequence of lack of balance. When a dog's
legs interfere, the rear leg on the forward swing hits the front leg on the same
side as it swings back (Fig. 2.11). A dog whose legs interfere may begin to pace

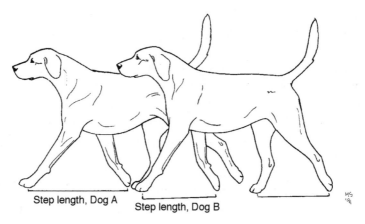

Step length, Dog A

Step length, Dog B

Fig. 2.10. The more angulation (Dog A), the greater the stride (step) length.

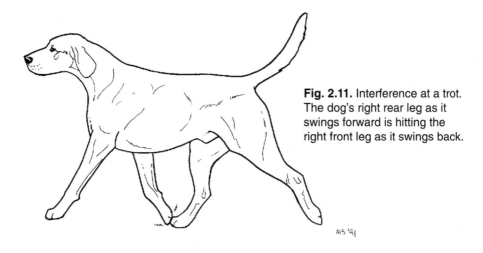

Fig. 2.11. Interference at a trot. The dog's right rear leg as it swings forward is hitting the right front leg as it swings back.

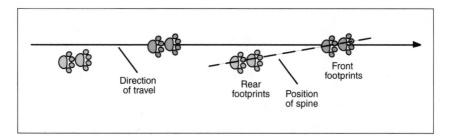

Direction of travel

Rear footprints

Position of spine

Front footprints

Fig. 2.12. A dog whose legs interfere may swing the rear legs to one side, causing crabbing, or sidewinding. The result is that the spine is angled with respect to the direction of travel.

in order to avoid interference. When a dog is pacing, there is no chance of interference since both legs on the same side move forward together.

Another way of compensating for lack of balance is crabbing, or sidewinding. A dog that crabs swings its rear to the right or the left so that the front and rear legs move in different planes. This prevents the front and rear feet on the same side from hitting each other. When a crabbing dog is viewed from above, the spine is not moving in a straight line, but is angled with respect to the direction of travel (Fig. 2.12).

Too little or too much angulation can be a problem for performance dogs. Minimal angulation results in stability. The most stable leg would be one that is completely straight, like the pillars that support the roof of a building. That is why dogs such as the Mastiff, Chow Chow, and Shar-Pei, originally bred as sentries to stand their ground against intruders, have less angulation. However, dogs with less angulated legs do not cover much ground at the trot. At the opposite extreme are breeds like the German Shepherd Dog which have a great deal of angulation. Their angulation allows them to cover a great deal of ground with each stride. Excessive angulation can be a problem, however. Limbs with excessive angulation may lack stability, causing them to hit as they swing past each other (Fig. 2.13).

Poor structure can seriously impede more complex forms of locomotion such as jumping. The musculature and angulation of the front and rear legs are crucial in providing power and spring for takeoff and cushioning the landing when jumping. Since different breed standards require different degrees of angulation, it is easier for some breeds to jump than others. During jumping, reach is particularly important because a dog must extend its front legs far forward when landing to reduce concussion (Fig. 2.14). A dog with a straight front will land with the leg in a more vertical position and thus will experience greater concussion upon landing. For such a dog, repeated jumping may cause undue pressure on the bones, joints, and soft tissues of the forelimb which would predispose the dog to elbow and shoulder injuries and degenerative joint disease.

In general, the rear legs are thought to be of prime importance for propulsion in running and jumping. Cineradiographic (slow motion moving radiographs) studies of dogs while running and jumping have demonstrated that the front legs can also provide a great deal of propulsion, especially the vertical propulsion needed for jumping. Full flexion and extension of the rear legs is also needed for efficient jumping. This is why animals with hip dysplasia, which

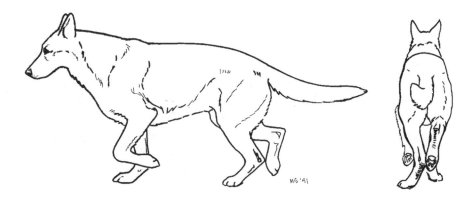

Fig. 2.13. Limbs with excessive angulation may lack stability, causing them to hit as they swing past each other.

M. Johanis

Fig. 2.14. Reach is very important for jumping because a dog must extend its front legs far forward when landing to reduce concussion.

reduces freedom of motion in the hip joint, may have limited propulsive ability. To compensate for the lack of forward propulsion these dogs may flip their hindquarters sideways as they jump. Such a twisting motion during jumping can make a dog susceptible to forelimb and spinal problems.

This chapter has presented only a brief introduction to locomotion and the effects of different types of structure on movement. For more details on this subject, the reader should refer to the books listed below.

Reading List

Rachel Page Elliot. *The New Dogsteps*. Howell Book House, NY, 1983.

Edward M. Gilbert, Jr. and Thelma R. Brown. *Canine Structure & Terminology*. Howell Book House, New York, 1995.

M. Christine Zink and Julie Daniels. *Jumping From A to Z: Teach Your Dog to Soar*. Canine Sports Productions, Lutherville, MD, 1996.

The selection of a performance dog is like any other talent search. The risk of disappointment is greater with young puppies, but many people love the challenge.

3.

SELECTING A

PERFORMANCE DOG

The best way to get a puppy is to beg for a baby brother — and they'll settle for a puppy every time.
Wilson Pendelton

One of the functions of a coach is to recognize and recruit talented players for the team. The coach may utilize the services of a talent scout, a specialist in spotting athletes with potential. Likewise, a person choosing a puppy for performance should take the time to hunt for a puppy that best suits the activities in which it will participate. It also may be helpful to enlist the services of an experienced breeder, handler, or judge.

NATURE VERSUS NURTURE

Environment

For centuries, we have argued the question of nature versus nurture. What factors make us who we are? Do we have artistic talent because of the genetic information passed on to us by our parents? Or does talent come from youthful experiences that influenced the way we perceive things? Many physical features in dogs and humans are easily explained on a genetic basis, but abilities in the area of intellect and performance are more difficult to explain. For centuries, scientists have studied identical twins who have been separated at birth. Since identical twins have exactly the same genetic makeup, differences between twins separated at birth can be attributed to differences in their environments. Still, although there have been numerous such studies, the question of genes versus environment, or nature versus nurture, has not been resolved.

Studies of monkeys have added fuel to the nature versus nurture question and have demonstrated that it can be very difficult to separate hereditary traits from the effects of environment. Decades ago, some newborn monkeys were separated from their mothers and from other young monkeys and raised for the first year of their lives with human companionship only. These monkeys were then placed with other monkeys of the same age, but for the remaining 25 years of their life, they were never normal. They were always fearful, and they were self-destructive, chewing and biting on themselves. They also tended to perform self-comforting, repetitive motions such as rocking themselves. In fact, they exhibited many behaviors of autistic children. When the monkeys died of old age, their brains were examined, and it was found that the internal anatomy of their brains was very different than that of the brains of normally reared monkeys. These studies suggested that nurture can actually change nature and that environment can actually determine and change anatomy — something previously believed to be strictly hereditary. These studies emphasize the importance of environmental influences on the cognitive development of any animal, regardless of whether it is a human, a monkey, or a dog.

Many of us, when given the opportunity to select a puppy or a kitten from a litter, have made the mistake of choosing the one that was most pathetic-looking — the puppy that seemed so forlorn, sitting in the corner of the box, while all its littermates played with potential buyers. As the animal grew, we probably noticed some abnormal behaviors, such as exaggerated fear of sounds or difficulty in adapting to new environments. Perhaps we blamed ourselves for not training it properly.

A friend of mine who wanted to get a puppy happened to see a six-month-old sable Shetland Sheepdog at a dog show. It was in a pen by itself with a sign advertising it for sale. She reached into the pen, and the puppy, already an adolescent, scuttled away from her. My friend bought that puppy and for six years tried to compete with it in obedience trials. It was obvious that Roy was very intelligent and could learn quickly. He loved to retrieve, and he was very agile. But no matter how much my friend tried to acclimatize him to the circumstances of dog shows, Roy was never able to compete in trials. He could never cope with the new conditions that he met at each show site. Roy's littermate, Ryan, who looked very similar and was also very smart became an excellent competitive obedience dog. Ryan was purchased at 7 weeks of age and socialized as a puppy, giving him adaptive skills. In this case, early environmental influences appear to have contributed significantly to Roy's inability to reach his potential in obedience.

The environment, especially during youth, has a significant influence on an animal's development. As soon as an animal is born, environmental stimuli begin to contribute to who that animal is and what its behavior will be. Performance dogs must be temperamentally and emotionally stable, because they will be placed under a certain amount of stress throughout their active lives as they attend competitive events. They will travel by car or airplane, visit new places, and encounter new people. They will be handled by strangers and asked to perform physically under a variety of different circumstances. Throughout their performance careers, they will need to fall back on both sound genetic temperament and the emotional strength that comes from an adequate upbringing.

Genetics

Having established the importance of environment in the development of a performance puppy, one must not underestimate the significance of genetics. Obviously, genetics are responsible to a large extent for the physical structure of a dog. But genetics also play a role in other, less obvious attributes of the performance dog, such as retrieving or herding instinct, intelligence, energy level, and willingness to please humans. Labrador Retrievers from field trial lines retrieve as soon as they can walk. Certainly a trait which is manifested at such a young age and without any training must be genetic. While a Belgian Sheepdog may not retrieve at three weeks of age, it may show an interest in herding small animals such as its littermates. Therefore, it would seem that the ability to herd is also genetically determined.

Although it is difficult to objectively measure intelligence in dogs, longtime breeders of dogs for performance events insist that intelligence, or at least the ability to learn quickly, is largely a hereditary trait. Guide Dogs for the Blind in San Rafael, California and other organizations that train assistance dogs have also found that there are individual differences in dogs' abilities to be trained, and that when the most able dogs are bred, they pass that trainability to their offspring.

THE STAGES OF DEVELOPMENT

A newborn puppy is very immature physiologically. At birth, the puppy can neither see nor hear. Several of the body systems are still developing and do not yet have a complete complement of functions. One of the most important partially developed systems is the nervous system. From the moment a puppy is born, and for the first few months of its life, the nervous system is taking in and processing information about the puppy's environment. As the puppy grows, the nervous system matures, permitting the puppy to have a wider range of movement to explore the environment and allowing it to learn from its environment at a faster rate. Experiences in the first few months of a puppy's life become ingrained and can have a permanent impact on the dog's future personality and behavior. Puppies pass through several universally recognized stages as they mature.

The Neonatal Period

This period lasts from birth until approximately two weeks of age. Puppies are born with their eyes shut and with their ears sealed. Their experience of the environment is obtained totally through the senses of touch and smell. During this time, the puppies move around by crawling, changing direction when they bump into objects. They are able to sense heat, cold, and texture and, given the opportunity, will choose a location with their optimal temperature. They are totally dependent on the bitch to feed them and to help them eliminate by licking them to stimulate bowel and bladder function.

Despite the fact that they cannot yet walk, it is possible for an experienced eye to assess certain features of a puppy's physical makeup, especially on the first day after birth. A puppy at this age can be evaluated for the relative length of its neck, spine, and tail. Its head can be examined by a person experienced in the particular breed and evaluated for the width and length of muzzle relative to the rest of the skull. Some experienced breeders can evaluate limb angulation at this age as well.

The Transitional Period

In this period, which lasts from about 14 to 21 days of age, the puppy's nervous system undergoes very rapid development. The puppy's eyes and ears open, and its deciduous (baby) teeth begin to emerge. At first the puppy is able to see only larger objects and objects that are moving slowly, but gradually its vision becomes more acute. During this period, the puppy stands up, first on the front legs and then on the back legs, and takes its first steps. By three weeks of age, the puppy has become quite curious about its environment and will wander around the whelping box. At this time, it begins to interact with littermates socially and learns play behavior. At the end of this period, most puppies are able to lap food from a bowl, although they continue to nurse.

The Socialization Period

This period, which lasts from three to twelve weeks of age, is a time during which the puppy is rapidly learning about the environment (Fig. 3.1). The puppy at this age is incredibly impressionable, and both positive and

Fig. 3.1. A seven-week-old puppy explores its environment.

negative experiences during this stage can be recorded permanently in its memory. This is called the socialization period because a dog's primary relationships are formed during this period.

Social Development

Early in this period, from three to five weeks, the puppy learns to relate to its littermates and other dogs as pack members. The puppy chews and bites at its littermates and begins to demonstrate adult behaviors such as play-fighting and scruff-shaking. During this time, the bitch teaches her puppies the canine body language they must know if they are to get along with other dogs as adults.

In the middle of the socialization period, at about five to seven weeks, the puppy begins to interact more with people and begins to perceive them as members of his pack. Puppies who receive little or no human contact during this period may have lifelong difficulty relating to people. Seven weeks of age is thought by many breeders to be the ideal time for a puppy to go to its new home: its canine socialization skills should have developed sufficiently, and it is receptive to all of the new experiences associated with a move to a new environment. The exact age at which the puppy goes to its new home varies based on the personality of the puppy, the priorities of the breeder, the wishes of the buyer, and even state laws.

The eighth week of age is often called the fear period, because a bad experience during this time can be imprinted permanently on the puppy's mind. Many people feel that puppies should not be shipped by air during this week, because of the increased risk of a frightening experience.

From nine to twelve weeks of age, the puppy continues to develop its repertoire of responses to different environments and the people within those environments. The puppy spends a great deal of time exploring at this age, and it is very responsive to people. It loves to come running in response to its name at this age — but just wait a few weeks!

Physical Development

Between three and five weeks of age, the puppy's limbs and neural patterns are developing. Gait cannot be evaluated until about five or six weeks of age at the earliest. At six weeks of age, the puppy has a full repertoire of physical activities, although its movements are not yet refined. If properly handled, a puppy at this age is able to respond to a person's commands with simple movements.

During the socialization period, it is essential that the breeder provide the puppy with more than just a warm place to sleep and food to eat. To fully develop socially and emotionally, a puppy needs a stimulating environment and personal attention from humans. A stimulating environment can be provided by giving the puppy objects such as boxes or tunnels to walk over and through like a canine jungle-gym, and a variety of toys so that it can experience different tastes and textures. Good examples of personal attention for a young puppy include being picked up, stroked, and held in different positions. Older puppies love to play chase games (*Chase the Human* is particularly exciting!), and most puppies will show some desire to chase and pick up objects (but not always to bring them back). This can and should be taken advantage of at this age by play-training, since it will make retrieve training much easier later. At least some of the personal attention paid to the puppy should be one-on-one to allow the puppy to develop as an individual. The fact that the environment and socialization are so critical further underscores the importance of choosing the right breeder, who controls the puppy's environment for the first weeks of live.

SELECTING A PUPPY

There is a great deal of research to be done before the puppy buyer should even look at the puppies in a litter. In most cases, this research should be done long before the puppies are born, probably even before they are conceived.

Initial research should center around selecting the correct breed for the performance event(s) in which the puppy will participate. Some performance events, such as AKC hunting tests and herding tests, are open only to certain breeds, whereas conformation shows, obedience, agility, and tracking are open to any breed of dog and often to mixed breeds. Other factors to consider in the choice of a breed include tolerance for shedding, and the dog's size, energy level, temperament, trainability, appearance, and compatibility with your temperament and lifestyle.

A word about mixed breeds. A number of performance events are open to mixed breeds, and mixed breeds can make just as wonderful pets as purebred dogs. Many people believe that, in general, mixed breed dogs are healthier than purebred dogs, if only because their random breeding has lessened the chance of doubling up on defective genes. However, even if both parents of a mixed breed puppy are known, such a puppy is more of an unknown quantity with respect to its eventual size, appearance, temperament, intelligence, and activity level. It is analogous to a baseball coach trying to find a major league player on a kid's sandlot team. He may miss completely, or he may find another Lou Gehrig or Joe DiMaggio. In addition, people obtaining mixed breed puppies for performance events should remember that, unfortunately, they will be limited as to the number and types of events which they can enter. Nonetheless, mixed breed puppies are no less deserving of homes than purebred pups, and if the performance event you are most interested in allows mixed breed dogs to compete, by all means adopt a deserving soul.

Having selected a particular breed of dog, the prospective owner should read the breed standard and several books about the breed. There are books that detail the origins of most breeds and describe and picture famous dogs in the history of those breeds. Some of these books also discuss common hereditary health problems in the breed. The buyer should join the local breed or all-breed club. Dog clubs usually offer informative seminars, fun events, and social contact with people who love to talk about dogs and share their experiences. Breed clubs often consist of people who are dedicated to retaining the breed's characteristics and strengths. Frequently, they have a breeder referral service so that people who wish to purchase a puppy can be linked up with those who have puppies for sale. This referral system is probably the best way to buy a purebred dog. Certainly it entails much less risk than purchasing a puppy from a pet store (never a good idea) or through a newspaper advertisement (usually not a good idea). The buyer should also attend several performance events and arrange to talk to successful owners and breeders in their chosen breed. Generally, experienced handlers of performance dogs will be quite frank about the advantages and disadvantages of their particular breed(s). They may also have information on planned breedings, either their own or those of others. At first, the amount of information will seem overwhelming, but eventually it will sort itself out, and the buyer will begin to establish a list of attributes which are of greatest importance in a dog of that breed.

Genetics

The buyer must then select a breeder to work with in obtaining a puppy. The first step is to find a breeder whom you can trust and whose dogs you like (for any of a number of reasons). It is a sad fact that, wherever there is money to be made or fame to be achieved, there is deception and dishonesty. Some people breed dogs for money or for fame without consideration for the health of the dogs or the longterm welfare of the breed. Many of these people can be identified during discussions on genetic problems in the breed. Beware of breeders who claim that they have never had any genetic problems in their lines! Stay clear of breeders who do not check for common hereditary conditions in their breed. Be wary of those who tell you that their animals have been tested as free of certain hereditary conditions, but who cannot show you the original veterinary examination reports for animals on their premises and photocopies of reports for those not living with them, such as the sire or grandsire. The breeder should be able to provide specific information on the health background of the sire and dam of the litter and preferably should be cognizant of the health of dogs in the pedigree for several generations back. Sadly, there are many ways to falsify veterinary examination reports, and potential buyers must, in the end, rely to some extent on their "sixth sense" to choose the right breeder.

Every breed has some hereditary problems. The specific inheritance of each of these problems may not always be understood, but since these problems are passed from generation to generation in certain lines of dogs, they are considered to have a significant genetic component. Table 3.1 provides a list of some common breeds of dogs and some of their hereditary or breed-associated conditions.

This very incomplete list has been provided, not to single out certain breeds with problems, but to emphasize the fact that every breed has defective genes within its gene pool, just as humans do. There are tests available to detect some of these conditions, including hip dysplasia, elbow dysplasia, progressive retinal atrophy, and hereditary cataracts. In addition, there are national registries such as the Orthopedic Foundation for Animals (OFA) and the Canine Eye Registration Foundation (CERF) (Table 3.2) that provide certification that a dog has been examined by a qualified veterinarian and has been found to be free of

Table 3.1
Genetic and Breed-Associated Conditions
in Some Familiar Breeds

Breed	Genetic Conditions
American Cocker Spaniels	Cataracts Progressive retinal atrophy Idiopathic aggression
Border Collies	Hip dysplasia Collie eye anomaly Progressive retinal atrophy Epilepsy
Poodles	Cataracts Progressive retinal atrophy Hypothyroidism Sebaceous adenitis
Golden and Labrador Retrievers	Hip dysplasia Cataracts Progressive retinal atrophy Subvalvular aortic stenosis Epilepsy Hypothyroidism Allergies von Willebrand's disease
Rottweilers	Hip dysplasia Cataracts von Willebrand's disease Subvalvular aortic stenosis
German Shepherd Dogs	Hip dysplasia Elbow dysplasia Collagen dysplasia Immune disorders Pituitary dwarfism von Willebrand's disease
Shetland Sheepdogs	Hypothyroidism von Willebrand's disease Ocular colobomas
Doberman Pinschers	Hypothyroidism von Willebrand's disease Cardiomyopathy Wobbler syndrome

Table 3.2
Who to Call
The following groups provide information on conditions
that can affect performance, and supply lists of veterinarians
who can perform appropriate health checks.

Hip Dysplasia

Orthopedic Foundation for Animals
2300 Nifong Blvd.
Columbia, MO 65201
(314) 442-0418

PennHip
c/o International Canine Genetics
271 Great Valley Pkwy.
Malvern, PA 19355
(800) 248-8099

Elbow Dysplasia

Orthopedic Foundation for Animals

Ocular Disorders

Canine Eye Registration Foundation
1235 SCC-A
Purdue University
W. Lafayette, IN 47907-1235
(317) 494-8179

Cardiac Conditions

American College of Veterinary Internal
    Medicine (Cardiology)
7175 West Jefferson Ave.
Suite 2125
Lakewood, CO 80235
(303) 980-7136

hereditary conditions. However, for some conditions, such as epilepsy, a buyer must rely on the honesty of the breeder to reveal whether any of the puppy's ancestors have suffered from the condition. Epilepsy is disheartening for breeders and puppy buyers alike since evidence of the condition may not surface until the dog is three or four years old, an age when the dog may already have been bred. Still other hereditary conditions of the dam and sire, such as entropion (eyelids that are folded inward, causing damage to the cornea), may not be evident to a buyer since they can be corrected surgically. Breeding a dog that has been surgically altered to correct or disguise a hereditary condition is highly unethical. Once again, the buyer must develop a relationship with the breeder that will permit honest discussion and the free exchange of information.

Physical Characteristics

The puppy being purchased as a potential performance dog should be carefully evaluated for structure. At seven weeks of age, most puppies give a fairly good indication of what they will look like as adults, both standing and moving. A well-known breeder of Golden Retrievers always said that one should evaluate a puppy at seven weeks and then not look at it again until it is two years of age. Although a puppy may go through a variety of stages in which it seems to alternately be all body and then all legs, by two years of age, the dog will usually regain the proportions that it had when it was seven weeks of age (Fig. 3.2). The puppy can be stacked (presented in a standing position as for the breed ring) and front and rear angulation, length of back, topline, tailset, and shape of head can all be evaluated. Ideally, you should bring an experienced judge, breeder, or puppy evaluator along to examine the litter before choosing a puppy. Bring someone who has examined many puppies and compared their initial impressions with the characteristics of the grown dog. Such a person can be an incomparable source of information. The breeder may provide additional information based on his/her experience with the specific lines involved and with the individual puppies in the litter.

Stack your puppy and evaluate it as if it were in the conformation ring (Fig. 3.3). One way to stack a puppy is to first swing it gently up and down in an arc in front of you, then place it on a slip-proof table. The puppy will be a little dizzy and will stand still, trying to regain its balance, while you stack it. Then take photos from side, front, and rear for a permanent record. When the puppy is an adult, it will have much the same structure as when it was a puppy (Fig. 3.4). Look for adequate shoulder layback and rear angulation. Shoulder layback is of utmost importance in performance dogs. Good shoulder layback allows for good reach of the front legs in running and jumping and contributes to agility and endurance by helping absorb concussion and impact. Adequate front and rear angulation also helps the dog to cover more ground with each stride.

Examine the puppy's gait from the side, front, and rear (Fig. 3.5). Generally a puppy will trot to follow a person who is enticing it. An experienced eye can detect the desirable, free-moving, balanced gait in a trotting puppy. In most breeds, the puppy should be showing a tendency to single-track without interference. Faults such as the legs moving too close to each other, elbows that swing out, or cowhocks can often be detected at this young age.

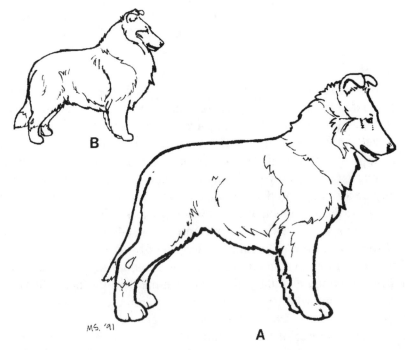

MS. '91

Fig. 3.2. A puppy at seven weeks of age (A) can be examined for certain structural characteristics such as the length of its back, the proportion of rib to loin, and the angulation of the legs. As an adult (B), the individual shows the same structural characteristics.

A puppy that is being chosen for a career in the conformation ring should be examined closely for its potential to approximate the breed standard as an adult. The breed standard should be read and studied carefully, and the buyer should get help from a breeder or judge in understanding the cryptic parts of some standards. For example, the Golden Retriever standard states that the hocks should be "well let down." Being a master of the English language will not help you understand what that means! Since there are no perfect examples of any breed, you usually must choose a dog that has minor imperfections because it has other, outstanding characteristics. Each person stresses specific traits that he/she believes are more important than others. Two people evaluating a litter of puppies may choose different puppies as their pick of the litter because of this personal conviction. One person may feel that the puppy with the lovely head and perfect ear set is the pick puppy, while another may select a puppy with a less outstanding head but one that has good shoulder layback and a solid topline.

There is no doubt that the best way to choose a dog for the conformation ring is to wait until it is older, preferably over nine months of age. At this age,

Fig. 3.3. A seven-week-old puppy is stacked for evaluation of front and rear angulation, length of back, topline, tailset, and head features.

Fig. 3.4. The same puppy as in Figure 3.3 at one year of age, showing the same ratio of height to length of back, and the same front and rear angulation.

Marcia Halliday

Fig. 3.5. A six-week-old puppy trotting.

you can have the dog examined (preliminarily) for the presence of certain hereditary conditions such as hip dysplasia and can be sure that the bite is correct. You can be reasonably sure that the dog will be within the appropriate size range, and, in males, that both of the testicles have descended and are normally positioned in the scrotum (a requirement for all male dogs shown in conformation). In addition, at this age, the dog is beginning to approximate its adult appearance. However, there are also disadvantages to getting an older dog. Young adult dogs with the specific attributes that you are looking for may be hard to find and expensive. Many people enjoy the antics of a puppy, and there is a definite bonding between dog and human that occurs early in puppyhood. In addition, some people would like to have more control over the dog's environment in those early, formative months. The right age at which to buy a puppy is often a matter of the buyer's priorities.

Within every litter of purebred puppies, there are a variety of body types. Different body types suit different performance events. Although the breed standard may state, for example, that the ideal specimen of a particular breed should be proportionately longer in body (the length from the point of the shoulder to the rear point of the buttocks) than it is tall (the height from the withers to the ground), a buyer who is interested in obtaining a puppy for obedience or agility may choose a puppy with a shorter back, because short-backed dogs are often more adept at controlling the placement of the rear legs, giving them an advantage in top-level obedience and agility competition. A friend of mine loves Cardigan Welsh Corgis and hunted for several months for a puppy with which to compete at the upper levels of obedience. She also wished to show the dog in conformation, but obedience was her first love. A top breeder offered her the pick of two litters, but she declined, as the dogs were very long-backed, even for this breed. Instead, she selected a puppy from a breeding that produced somewhat short-backed puppies (although still within the breed standard) and has been successful in both conformation and obedience. A person selecting a dog for field trials or hunting tests may choose a smaller, more wiry puppy, or one with a shorter, dense coat, since hunting dogs are required to run long distances and press through obstacles such as brush and brambles. Another person, who has little time or interest in grooming, may pick a puppy with a coat that will be easy to care for.

Temperament

Physical structure is much easier to evaluate objectively than temperament. Evaluating the temperament of a puppy is a subjective, or individual, matter. Individual people prefer certain characteristics of temperament in a dog. Some people prefer a dog that shows signs of independence. They would choose a puppy who is off playing by himself or perhaps running away to investigate new circumstances (Fig. 3.6) and then returning to the litter periodically. Others prefer a puppy that focuses totally and entirely on them. They may choose a puppy who sits and watches them for long periods of time. The energy level of puppies can also be evaluated. Most people who purchase puppies for athletic events know that their dogs will need stamina and pick an energetic puppy. But despite all of these evaluations, it should be noted that a given puppy on any day can exhibit atypical characteristics either because the puppy is tired or just is not feeling at its peak that day.

Fig. 3.6. Some people prefer puppies that are independent, venturing away from the litter to investigate and periodically checking in.

Puppy Temperament Testing

There are several simple tests that can be performed on puppies at about seven weeks of age to assess temperament. The purpose of these tests is to evaluate the puppies so that they can best be matched to the buyer's needs, experience, and lifestyle. A shy, quiet person may wish to buy a quiet, loving, somewhat submissive puppy. A more aggressive person who wants a top-notch obedience dog may choose a more dominant puppy with a high energy level (although an overly dominant or aggressive puppy would not be suitable either). An example of a series of puppy temperament tests is presented here. These tests are not of the true or false variety, which have only black and white answers. Instead, they give an indication of a puppy's degree of dominance and independence, its desire to please, and its ability to cope with changes or new stimuli in the environment. Because the puppies are tested individually, away from their littermates, they may demonstrate behaviors that were not evident in the context of the litter.

Anyone can perform temperament tests on puppies, but because the tests are subjective, they are best performed by someone who has experience in interpreting puppy behavior. In addition, they should be performed by a person who is a stranger to the puppies and in a location where the puppies have never been, so that the puppies will have no previous associations that might affect the test results. The puppies should be awake but not tired when tested, and they should not be tested right after having eaten. It is fascinating to see the variety of responses which different puppies may have to the same stimuli. For more detail, the reader should refer to *Behavior Problems in Dogs,* by William E. Campbell and *How to Raise a Puppy You Can Live With,* by David H. Neil and Clarice Rutherford.

Temperament Tests

1. *Recall Test:* The tester kneels down and when the puppy is looking, quietly claps her hands together while calling the puppy. The tester should use happy, repetitive words such as, "Puppy, puppy, puppy." A puppy that is very independent and indifferent or shy of humans will not come (Fig. 3.7), whereas a puppy that is attracted to people will come and perhaps jump up and lick the tester.

2. *Stroking Test:* The tester strokes the puppy from head to tail for about 30 seconds. A puppy that bites the tester's hand during this procedure is a more aggressive puppy, while one that jumps up and licks the tester's hand demonstrates interest in people and eagerness to please. A puppy that rolls over during this procedure is very submissive, and one that runs away is showing independence, disinterest, or fear.

Fig. 3.7. A puppy that is shy of humans may not be confi-
dent enough to come when called encouragingly.

3.   *Restraint Test:* The tester rolls the puppy over on its back on the ground
     and holds it down with the palm of the hand. In another similar test, the
     puppy is held by the abdomen in the tester's hands, with its legs hanging
     down but not touching the ground. A puppy that struggles continuously
     and growls or bites in an attempt to be freed is showing dominance. A
     passive puppy will not struggle at all. A feisty puppy who is well social-
     ized to humans will be more likely to struggle and then submit.

4.   *Following Test:* The tester walks past the puppy within a foot or two,
     being sure that the puppy sees her. With the puppy watching, the tester
     walks away. The object is to see whether the puppy follows. Try this
     test several times if the puppy doesn't immediately follow. A puppy that
     follows shows a desire to interact with humans, whereas one that fails to
     follow, even after several tries, may be very independent and not strongly
     oriented to humans.

5.   *Retrieving Test:* The tester makes a ball from a piece of paper and teases
     the puppy with it, then tosses it past the puppy about three feet away,
     making sure that the puppy sees it. A puppy that chases the ball shows
     that it can pay attention and that it has some retrieving, or at least chas-
     ing, instinct. A puppy that brings it back has a strong retrieving instinct
     and a desire to work with and for people. Many trainers of obedience
     and field dogs place great weight on this test, as they have found that
     dogs which will chase the ball and readily retrieve to a person also make
     excellent obedience or field dogs.

6.   *Pinch Test:* The tester pinches the skin between the puppy's toes softly
     at first and then gradually increases the pressure, noting when the puppy

responds. A puppy that yelps loudly and continuously after a light pinch is very pain sensitive. One that licks the tester and tries to make up has a forgiving nature and will likely be easier to train. This test is also widely used by people training field and obedience dogs.

7.   *Sound Test:* The tester stands several feet from the puppy and bangs on a pot with a metal spoon, then drops the pot with the spoon in it. A puppy that is initially startled, then walks over to investigate, is showing curiosity and the ability to adjust to distressing environmental stimuli. One that is very startled and refuses to investigate may be sound sensitive and is not assertive enough to overcome its fear of the object. It should be noted, however, that the validity of this test is not universally accepted. Many puppies that appear sound sensitive in this test are not sound sensitive as adults. In fact, the majority of dogs that fail to become dog guides at Guide Dogs for the Blind do so because of sound sensitivity. This is despite the fact that this organization has experience in temperament testing over 7,000 puppies — more than any single breeder could (or should) produce in a lifetime.

There are many responses to these tests other than the few discussed here. It may be necessary to choose a puppy that has a less than desirable response in one area because of the overall responses of the puppy to the other tests. For example, a person choosing a puppy for obedience may pick a puppy that was somewhat sound sensitive during the puppy tests because it willingly retrieved, was most attentive, and was the puppy that showed the most responsiveness to people. Temperament tests can also give the buyer information as to the areas in which the dog will need to be given extra socialization and experience as it grows.

The breeder can be an invaluable source of information regarding the temperament of individual puppies. The breeder knows the temperament of the sire and dam, has been observing the puppies since birth, and knows their responses to many different environmental stimuli (Fig. 3.8). In addition, the breeder knows the types of temperament that are produced by individuals in the breeding program. For example, I had a Golden Retriever, Cajun, who had what I consider to be excellent temperament for performance activities. As Cajun got older and I was ready for another puppy, I wanted one with temperament just like Cajun. The breeder of Cajun's sire, Robbie, told me that Robbie frequently produced puppies with temperament like Cajun's, regardless of the bitch he was bred to. I got another puppy sired by Robbie, (who was by then 12 years old), and my puppy turned out to be just like a little Cajun in a female body.

Fig. 3.8. The breeder, who knows the temperaments of the sire and dam and their previous offspring, can be a valuable source of information, helping to predict the temperament of the puppies.

Gender

Many people find the question of whether to acquire a male or a female puppy a difficult one. Often those with minimal experience have preconceived ideas about the temperament and behavior of male and female dogs. These ideas are fostered by some veterinarians who routinely advise their clients to obtain female dogs because they believe that females have fewer behavioral problems. Although males and females do tend to have certain gender-associated characteristics, these are influenced by the breed of the dog, hereditary factors, individual differences, training, and neutering.

Physically, male dogs are usually taller and heavier boned. They tend to have larger, more impressive heads and, in coated breeds, they have longer, denser coats. Intact males of some breeds have a tendency to be more aggressive toward other intact male dogs and may be more likely to roam. Of course, this should not be a problem because all dogs should be confined unless they are supervised. Male dogs tend to have a more constant activity level. Females have a tendency to be quieter and more focused. They may be moody, especially around the time of their heat cycles, and at this time, some females have a lower energy level.

Many people perceive male dogs as dominant and females as more passive and affectionate, but in many multidog households, a female is usually the dominant member of the dog pack, having strong control over the sometimes browbeaten males. The dominance of the female may be carried over into relationships with people in the household. Often males are more affectionate and passive, while females challenge for the leadership role.

There are also breed-related differences in male and female temperament and behavior. For example, both males and females of the terrier breeds will have a tendency to be more aggressive toward other dogs than either gender of more passive breeds such as the Newfoundland or the Labrador Retriever. This is not a matter of bad temperament in terriers, but reflects the original purpose of these breeds, which was to ferret out vermin. This activity required boldness, which was intentionally bred into the terriers. Similarly, male dogs of some of the larger Working breeds such as the Great Pyrenees and Rottweiler may be more aggressive than males of some of the Sporting breeds like the Golden Retriever or the Clumber Spaniel.

Hereditary factors can sometimes override gender in determining temperament and behavior. Within any given breed, certain stud dogs and bitches consistently produce puppies with specific characteristics of temperament. Some may produce very smart and attentive puppies with bold, outgoing temperaments, regardless of gender. Other dogs, unfortunately, have developed a reputation for producing puppies with aggressive temperaments where this trait is considered undesirable.

In addition, most, if not all, objectionable gender-associated behaviors can be modified by training. For example, no one needs to put up with a male dog mounting the legs of family members or house guests. Simple obedience training, applied with consistency, can put an end to these and most other unwanted behaviors permanently.

Finally, spaying or neutering can significantly modify gender-related temperament characteristics. The decision to spay or neuter must be approached individually for every dog. Spaying or neutering does modify the behavior of a dog, especially if the procedure is done at an early age before bad habits are allowed to develop. In general, neutering (castration) makes male dogs less aggressive toward other males and, of course, decreases their interest in female dogs. Spaying (ovariohysterectomy) prevents a female dog from experiencing the physical and hormonal changes and unwanted attention associated with heat cycles. Spaying or neutering does not cause a dog to become overweight, but the dog may require less food to maintain its body weight and therefore is more likely to be overfed. It should be noted, however, that neutering a young male dog can cause it to grow taller than it would if left intact until after the growth plates have closed. Testosterone helps to close the growth plates, and if the testosterone is removed by neutering, the dog usually grows taller.

There are definite health benefits to spaying and neutering. Females that are spayed before their first heat cycle have a significantly reduced risk of mammary cancer later in life and will not develop infections of the uterus (pyometra), which can be life-threatening. Neutered males have a reduced risk of prostatic enlargement or infection, a condition often seen in older dogs.

The particular performance event planned for a show dog's career may influence whether a dog can be spayed or neutered. Dogs that will be shown in conformation cannot be altered, but spayed or neutered dogs may participate in most of the other performance events. There are many people who believe that a certain gender is more suited to a particular performance event. For example, many obedience trainers feel that male dogs are best for obedience competition because they are less likely to be stressed by strong physical corrections. However, there have been a number of top-notch female obedience dogs, and it is my belief that a female dog is not inferior to a male but may require a different, perhaps less physical kind of training. There is no doubt, however, that the heat cycles in an unaltered female can reduce the amount of time that the dog can participate in performance events such as obedience and field trials, in which females in heat may not participate. This is a significant disadvantage to those who campaign a dog throughout the year, and most people find it advantageous to spay a female dog soon after the decision has been made not to breed her. Owners of intact male dogs may find the decision of whether to neuter a little more difficult. Some people believe that the male hormones help a dog maintain its stamina in athletic competitions and resist neutering for that reason. In the end, the decision of whether to spay or neuter a dog must be made based on the behavior, health, temperament, and performance requirements of each individual dog.

THE BUYER'S RESPONSIBILITIES

Once you get your puppy home, the work really begins. You are now completely responsible for this little being who will, it is hoped, be your companion for over a decade. The owner of a performance dog must ensure that the puppy has everything it needs to develop into a well-adjusted adult, including health care, excellent nutrition, exercise, socialization, and training. You should

Fig. 3.9. A puppy being exposed to some of the tools of the trade.

(carefully) provide your puppy with as many different experiences as possible, including meeting new people and other dogs of all ages, traveling in a car, going to new locations such as large buildings and noisy shopping areas, and spending quality time alone with you. You should also provide your puppy with early exposure to the tools of its trade, such as brushes, combs, nail clippers, bumpers, pigeon wings, water (Fig. 3.9), dumbbells, gloves, and baby gates. The new puppy is a blank book in which you can write.

SELECTING AN ADULT FOR PERFORMANCE

There are definite advantages to selecting an adult dog for performance. One of the greatest advantages is that the adult dog is a known quantity with respect to size, conformation, and temperament. These dogs may have been screened for genetic diseases such as hip dysplasia and cataracts. The adult dog can begin training immediately — no need to wait out all of those stages which a puppy goes through (and often no house training!). Many professional trainers of dogs for movies and television shows select their dogs from animal shelters. One such person has devised a set of tests he finds extremely helpful in selecting adult dogs to be trained as movie stars. He first approaches the dog while it is penned. He prefers that the dog just sit or stand there, looking at him while he approaches. This is an indication that the dog has a high level of acceptance towards humans. He then tests the dog's sight and hearing. He throws an object past the dog's head and checks to see if the dog watches it, and he makes a noise to see if the dog responds to it. He then does a test for pain tolerance by squeezing the webbing of the dog's foot. He would like the dog to be very tolerant of pain. (Other people might desire a different level of pain tolerance.) If the dog has passed all of these tests, he then tests its reaction to food. Because he uses food to train his dogs, he wants the dog to show an interest in getting a snack even after it has been offered for the twentieth time. He finds that 90 percent of dogs that pass all of these tests will be successful on the movie set. A similar, or somewhat modified, set of temperament tests can be devised by a person seeking an adult performance dog.

Sometimes a dog purchased as an adult can be taken on speculation. A trial period of several weeks may be set up so that the purchaser can spend time with the dog and see whether it is suitable. During this period, health checks such as hip and eye evaluations may also be performed.

Reading List

David H. Neil, Clarice Rutherford. *How to Raise a Puppy You Can Live With.* Alpine Press, Loveland, CO, 1992.

William E. Campbell. *Behavior Problems in Dogs.* American Veterinary Publishers, Santa Barbara, CA, 1975.

Clarence J. Pfaffenberger. *The New Knowledge of Dog Behavior.* Howell Book House, New York, NY, 1963.

Dogs need regular care to perform at their peak.

4.

ROUTINE MAINTENANCE

OF THE PERFORMANCE DOG

The average dog is a nicer person than the average person.
Andy Rooney

A performance dog, like a human athlete, must be in peak physical condition to perform at its potential. A regular program of routine maintenance will help prevent physical and medical problems and will facilitate early detection of problems that do occur. This chapter describes routine procedures that you should perform to keep your teammate tuned up and ready to go.

MAINTENANCE PROCEDURES

Teeth

Periodontal disease is by far the most common disease of the teeth in dogs, reported by some to be present in about 95% of dogs over 2 years of age. The cause of periodontal disease in dogs is the same as for humans — buildup of plaque and calculus on the teeth, leading to gingivitis. You should regularly examine your dog's teeth for the presence of calculus. Dogs fed soft diets (semi-moist or canned food) have a higher incidence of periodontal disease than those fed dry food.

Periodontal disease starts with the adhesion of oral bacteria to remnants of saliva on the surface of the tooth. The bacteria proliferate, particularly in crevices and other irregularities on the surface of the tooth, and their by-products produce plaque. The plaque then becomes calcified by calcium salts that are present in saliva, forming calculus, or tartar. Calculus is a hard white, yellow, or brown material on the surface of the tooth, particularly close to the gum line. Calculus permits bacteria to replicate in a pocket between the gum and the tooth. These bacteria produce chemicals that irritate the gums, resulting in gingivitis. As gingivitis progresses, the inflammatory reaction begins to erode the bone that holds the tooth in place. The tooth then becomes loose and may fall out as the bone recedes more and more.

Prevention is the key to beating periodontal disease. The best preventative is tooth brushing. It may seem strange to think of brushing a dog's teeth, but many people do it. I have a friend whose German Shepherd puppy was always fascinated when she went into the bathroom to brush her teeth. He would stand up with his front legs on the sink to get a closer look. So just for fun, she started to take a couple of swipes across his teeth with an old toothbrush. When she learned of the benefits of tooth brushing in dogs, she started doing it routinely, even using human toothpaste. It is not necessary to use toothpaste at all, but there are meat-flavored toothpastes available for dogs. I realize that not everyone has the time or the inclination to brush his/her dog's teeth, but it is definitely the best way to maintain healthy teeth.

Studies have shown that dogs that chew regularly on either rawhide chips or hard biscuits have significantly less plaque. So if you don't brush your dog's teeth, providing a small rawhide chip once or twice each day may be the next best thing. In addition, there are a number of chew toys on the market that do a credible job of reducing plaque. Some may even remove calculus in the most vigorous chewers. These toys have bumps over their surfaces. As the dog chews, the bumps become rough and scrape the surface of the dog's teeth. Note that rawhide chewtoys and other toys can be dangerous. Always supervise your dog when chewing a rawhide, as they can cause choking. Test toys on your dog before leaving him alone with them. Aggressive chewers could break some of them into pieces small enough to cause choking.

Calculus can be removed using a dental tool that can be purchased at most kennels or pet supply outlets. Place your dog on its side and pull the lips up, exposing the teeth. Your dog will be more comfortable if you wet your hands frequently while working on its teeth. The upper teeth can easily be seen with the dog's mouth closed. To work on the lower teeth, it helps to place a ball in your dog's mouth to hold it open. Press the dental tool against the tooth at its junction with the gum and pull down along the tooth. The calculus, which has formed a sort of cast around the tooth, will pull away from the tooth relatively

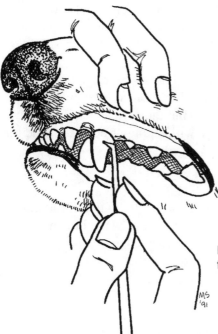

Fig. 4.1. Calculus can be manually removed from the teeth using a dental tool.

cleanly if enough pressure is applied (Fig. 4.1). Generally, a dog will take routine oral care in stride if its mouth is handled from puppyhood. Calculus can also be removed by a veterinarian using an ultrasonic descaler. Regardless of the method, appropriate follow-up is necessary to regain the health of the gums. If the gingivitis is not taken care of, the calculus will quickly re-form.

Dogs with damage to the valves of the heart, or who are being treated with corticosteroids or anti-inflammatory drugs, should receive broad-spectrum antibiotics just before and for several days after the teeth are scaled. Animals with these conditions are more susceptible to the development of systemic infections by oral bacteria that readily enter the blood stream through cuts in the gum.

Your dog's mouth should be examined periodically for broken teeth. If you find a broken tooth, push on it to see if it is loose. A loose tooth, or one with an exposed pulp cavity, may need to be extracted. If a tooth is infected, the dog will wince or jerk its head in pain when the tooth is pressed. An infected tooth should be treated by a veterinarian who will prescribe appropriate antibiotics, or perhaps extract the tooth if the infection is very advanced. You should also note the color of your dog's teeth. White teeth are generally healthy, whereas brown or gray teeth may have lost their blood supply and may be devitalized. It is normal for older dogs to have brown spots on the top of worn teeth, especially the incisors.

The gums should be examined for reddening (a sign of gingivitis) or areas of swelling. Older dogs may develop proliferations of the gum tissue, called epulis. These growths resemble tumors, but they are generally benign. If they grow large enough, they may interfere with eating or occlusion and may need to be removed surgically.

Ears

Examine the inside of your dog's ears periodically with a flashlight. Some dogs always have clean ears, although a little bit of waxy brown discharge is also normal. An ear that is simply dirty can be cleaned gently with a cotton ball dampened (not soaked) with a veterinary product that dissolves wax. The dog's ear canal is L-shaped, so there is little danger of breaking the eardrum by cleaning the ear in this manner.

Normal ears are not red or painful when touched and should not smell foul. Reddening of the ears, head-shaking, and/or a foul-smelling discharge are signs of otitis, or inflammation of the ear. If the infection doesn't respond in a few days to regular cleaning, it should be given veterinary attention, because these infections can progress to involve the deeper structures of the ear. Chronic otitis can cause hearing loss if left untreated.

Dogs with dropped ears, especially those that enjoy swimming, seem to be more susceptible to ear infections. Many yeast and fungal organisms thrive in slightly damp environments. In addition, the skin of the ear canal doesn't form a tight barrier against infection unless it is dry. Dogs with allergies are especially prone to ear infections, as are dogs with smaller ear canals and those that have hair growing deep within the ear canal. In susceptible breeds, it is helpful to cut away the hair around the opening to the ear canal (Fig. 4.2) and pluck the hair from the ear canal itself. This allows better air circulation so that the skin of the ear can stay dry. It also may help to sprinkle athletes' foot powder (which contains dry antifungal agents) into the ears after swimming, or even once a week during the spring and summer when most ear infections occur. Products with drying properties are usually preferable to oily products for treating ear infections.

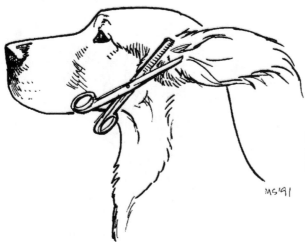

Fig. 4.2. Hair may be cut away from around the ear, permitting better circulation of air.

MS'91

Coat

Your dog's coat and skin should be examined weekly. He will think he's in seventh heaven as you rub your hands over his body, feeling for lumps and picking out small burrs or plant seeds which may have been missed when he was checked after that romp in the woods. Go over your dog's body carefully. It's very easy to miss a lump in an area where the coat is very thick or where you rarely touch. If you locate a lump, part the hair, and take a look at it. It may be a healing scab where you removed a tick several days ago or where a puppy's sharp teeth nicked the skin in play. If the lump is not a scab, but a raised area, pinch the skin and feel the lump between your fingers. Move the skin around with the lump held between your fingers. Record how big it is. If the lump seems to be attached to the tissue below, or if it is larger than a half inch, it should be checked by a veterinarian. Otherwise, check the lump each week, and if it grows or becomes attached to the tissue below, have it removed.

Foxtail awns can get entangled in the coat and cause significant problems. Foxtail awns are the seeds of the foxtail plant, a weed found on roadsides and in fields throughout the United States and Canada. The seed itself is tiny, but it has many large spikes on it, all of which point in the same direction (Fig. 4.3) and act like the barbs of a fish hook. They permit the foxtail awn to move in one direction but prevent it from coming back out.

I was taught in veterinary school that foxtail awns could be very dangerous because they could get into the nasal passages or lungs and cause infections. I always thought that it would be rare occurrence for a dog to inhale one of these

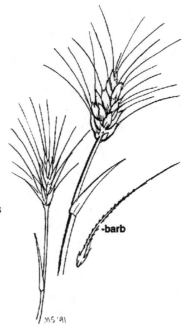

Fig. 4.3. Foxtail awns, showing the barbs present on each seed.

seeds so deeply that it would work its way down into the lungs. Then I got a Sporting dog with a very dense undercoat. I would frequently find foxtail awns in his coat after he had been running outdoors. They were always difficult to pull out, because the fine hairs of the undercoat had become enmeshed in the barbs of the seed. One day, as I was doing my dog's weekly checkup, I felt what I thought might be a tick, tightly adherent to the skin of his chest. When I parted the hair, I saw that it was a foxtail awn which was deeply embedded in the skin. This little seed was actually being driven through unbroken skin! I have since found this condition several other times. Once a foxtail awn has passed through the skin, it can work its way throughout the body. The combination of the barbs and the movement of the tissues continually move it in one direction. I know of one dog that had six separate surgical operations to treat abscesses and to attempt to locate and remove a single foxtail awn that had traveled through the lungs and several abdominal organs, finally exiting through the skin of one of the back legs. Each time the surgery was performed, the veterinarian was unable to find the offending seed, because it had already caused its damage and moved on before the infection became severe enough to require surgery. The dog suffered permanent damage to the lungs, liver, and intestines, all as a result of this one small seed.

Nails and Feet

The nails are very important to performance dogs. They provide traction while running and jumping and protect the bones of the foot and the pads and feet from damage. The nails and feet should be examined every week to check for excessive nail growth, for dirt or foreign bodies between the toes, and for cuts on the pads or the skin between the toes.

The nails grow at different speeds in individual dogs. Many dogs need to have their nails trimmed once a week. Some dogs, particularly those kept in concrete kennel runs or that run several miles a day on paved roads with their owners, wear their nails down sufficiently through these activities.

There is no doubt that nail trimming is one of the least pleasurable activities in a dog's life. However, if a dog has its nails trimmed often from the time it is a young puppy, and if the owner makes the experience as quick and as stress-free as possible (and maybe adds occasional treats throughout the process), most dogs will submit to the experience. An occasional dog will always be intractable when the nail clippers come out of the cupboard. I know of a Belgian Tervuren with its Championship, Utility Dog, and Tracking Dog titles, and multiple High in Trial obedience awards that was obedient at all times except when she saw the nail clippers. It always took two people to hold her down while her nails were cut. Luckily, such a dog is the exception rather than the rule.

The nails can be cut with a guillotine-type tool or nail cutters, which operate like scissors. Be sure that the nail cutting blade is sharp. Blades of the guillotine nail cutters can readily be replaced when they become dull. The scissors-type nail cutters have to be sent out for sharpening or the entire tool replaced. A dull blade crushes the nail as it cuts. In addition to being painful to the dog (there is a nerve that runs down the center of the nail), crushing can cause the nail to split, leaving cracks for dirt and microorganisms to enter and perhaps cause infection. Some people prefer to use a dremmel tool to grind the nails down. When using one of these tools, be sure to keep hair (yours and your dog's) out of the way. It takes only a split second for the hair to get wrapped up in the tool, causing serious damage to the skin and deeper tissues.

A blood vessel runs down the center of the nail. It is preferable to cut the nails as close to the blood vessel as possible, without making it bleed. In dogs with white nails, the vessel is easy to see, especially if the nail is held sideways up to a light. But for dogs with brown or black nails, there are two

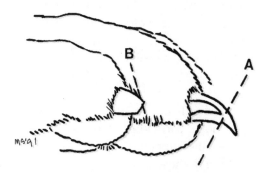

Fig. 4.4. Side view of a nail showing the location of the blood vessel. The nail should be cut just beyond the blood vessel (A). In dogs with large nails, a second cut can be made across the top of the nail (B).

Fig. 4.5. End view of a nail showing the white crescent that can be seen on the cut end of the nail just before the quick.

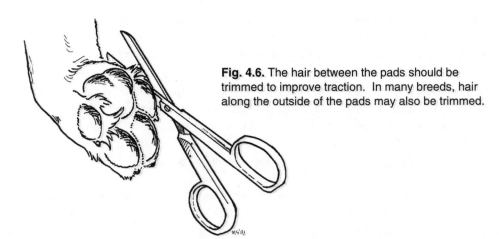

Fig. 4.6. The hair between the pads should be trimmed to improve traction. In many breeds, hair along the outside of the pads may also be trimmed.

other landmarks to determine how short to cut the nail. When looking at the nail from the side, you will see that it is initially wide and then suddenly becomes narrower (Fig. 4.4). The blood vessel usually stops at the junction of the wide and narrow parts. If you cut the nail about one millimeter beyond this point, it is unlikely that the vessel will be cut. If, after cutting at this point, a small, soft, white crescent can be seen on the cut end (Fig. 4.5), the nail has been cut short enough. If not, the nail should be cut shorter by taking off little shavings. The guillotine nail cutters are particularly useful for this. In dogs over forty pounds, a second cut across the top of the nail can also be made (Fig. 4.4). This helps to shorten the nail further without risking bleeding. Care should be taken when cutting dewclaws. Although these nails do not regularly contact the ground and therefore do not wear, the dewclaws seem to grow more slowly than the other nails and therefore may need to have less removed.

In coated breeds, the hair on the feet can grow very long and cover the pads, resulting in loss of traction. In addition, hair between the toes can become matted and accumulate plant matter, mud, and moisture. This is uncomfortable for the dog and may contribute to foot problems. The hair should be trimmed from around the edges of the pads and from between the pads (Fig. 4.6). This should be done carefully with blunt-ended scissors to prevent accidentally cutting the skin between the toes, which is especially soft. In some breeds, such as Salukis, Cavalier King Charles Spaniels, and Pekingese, it is customary to leave feathering around the edge of the foot.

Anal Glands

The anal glands are two small glands that empty their secretions into sacs just inside the skin below the anus; they are located at about 5 o'clock and 7 o'clock (Fig. 4.7). The sacs empty periodically via a small duct that extends from the sac, upwards towards the anus. The secretion has a distinctive odor that most people find unpleasant. These sacs are the dog's version of the scent glands of a skunk, although they do not smell quite so bad! Most dogs empty their anal glands on their own, usually when they defecate. Occasionally, a dog may involuntarily empty its anal glands when frightened.

A dog that is uncomfortable because of full anal sacs will scoot its rear on the ground, trying to empty them. The normal anal sac secretion is clear or pale yellow-brown. There should not be more than 0.5 mL (¼ teaspoon) in the anal sacs of a forty-pound dog. If there is an increased quantity, and if the material is thick and a dark brown or gray color, the anal gland may be impacted (unable to empty). Most dogs do not need to have their anal glands emptied

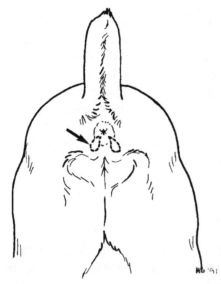

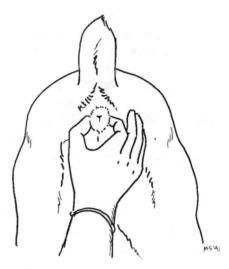

Fig. 4.7. The anal sacs (arrow indicates one) are located below the anal sphincter at five o'clock and seven o'clock and each one has a duct leading upward to an opening in the skin just beside the anal opening.

Fig. 4.8. External method for emptying the anal glands, especially useful in small dogs.

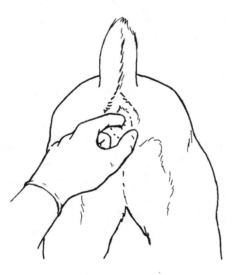

Fig. 4.9. Internal method for emptying the anal glands.

manually. Some dogs need them emptied during puberty, and others need them to be emptied once or twice a year or sometimes more often.

The general technique for emptying the anal glands is to squeeze the gland from the wide end toward the narrow end, forcing the secretion upwards and out the duct. There are two ways to empty anal glands. In the external method, a batt of cotton is held against the dog's anus. The area of the anal glands is squeezed between the thumb and forefingers, forcing the material to be expelled through the ducts and into the cotton batting (Fig. 4.8). This is the method of choice for very small dogs (under 20 pounds) and can also be used in larger dogs. The disadvantage of this method is that you cannot feel the anal sacs very well, so you cannot tell how full they are, nor whether they have emptied completely. In addition, some feel that this method is more painful to the dog than the internal method. In the internal method, a latex glove is worn and the index finger is lubricated with mineral oil or another safe lubricant. The index finger is inserted into the anus and is bent downwards, pinching the anal gland between the inserted finger and the thumb, which remains on the outside. When the gland is squeezed at the base, the contents are forced upwards through the duct to exit at the junction of the anus with the skin (Fig. 4.9). Each gland is emptied individually this way. The advantage of this technique is that the anal gland can be felt between the thumb and finger, making it easy to assess how big it is and whether it has been emptied completely. However, this technique is not suitable for very small dogs, and some people have an aversion to doing a rectal examination on a dog.

An anal gland abscess develops when there is a large buildup of secretion in the anal glands, and the lining of the sac becomes torn, exposing the tissue underneath to the anal gland secretion. The tissue around the gland may then become inflamed, swollen, and painful to the dog. The swelling may actually squeeze the duct shut so that more secretion accumulates. The secretion from an infected anal gland may be tan or yellow like pus, and gas (produced by bacteria in the infected gland) may escape when the gland is expressed. Infected anal glands should be treated by a veterinarian who can flush them with an appropriate antibiotic.

Weight

Our dogs depend on us to put food in their bowls. And, for many performance dogs, we are putting in too much. A large percentage of performance dogs are overweight; some are actually obese. These are not couch potato dogs. They are expected to jump in obedience, to run over rough ground in retrieving tests, and to traverse agility obstacles. The sad results of overweight performance dogs are ruptured anterior cruciate ligaments (often both legs), severe arthritis in dogs in their prime, degenerative disk disease, and many more conditions that are caused, or exacerbated by, excess weight. Why are so many working dogs overweight? These are some possible answers to this complex question:

1. Keeping a dog at working weight may be incompatible with winning in conformation shows.

I have never understood why dogs whose breed standard states that they should be shown in "hard working condition" don't win in the conformation ring unless they are fat. The only thing I can think of is that we are mistaking fat for muscle. In the meantime, for breeds such as Golden Retrievers and Labrador Retrievers, assume that if your dog is winning in the conformation ring, it is probably about 8 to 15 pounds overweight. When you are finished showing your dog in conformation, take the weight off — for his longterm health.

2. People are feeding their adult dogs the same amount of food they were fed as adolescents.

This is a common mistake. But just as most of us eat less now than we did as teenagers, your dog needs less, too. A dog's metabolism slows down with age, and adult dogs need less food to maintain their weight.

3. People believe the suggested feeding regimens on the dog food bag.

Even the most active dog doesn't need as much food as most dog food companies recommend. To determine how much food a dog needs, feed it the amount that maintains its weight.

4. The dog has been less active, but he is still being fed the same amount of food.

Adjust your dog's intake to his activity level. Remember that in the winter, your dog may not get as much exercise, and decrease his intake accordingly. Every time you go to the dog food bag, think about how much exercise your dog has had that day, and dole out an appropriate amount of food.

5. People don't know how to determine the correct weight for their dogs.

Dogs vary in height, bone structure, and muscularity, so there is no one correct weight for a dog of any given breed. The best way to determine whether a dog is overweight is to check three different parts of the body: the neck, the ribs, and the hips. Just like humans, individual dogs may carry the majority of their weight in one particular area, so you need to check all three sites.

a) To check the neck, press your thumb and index finger deep into the side of the neck just ahead of the shoulder and pinch them together. If your fingers are

Fig. 4.10. Although many people might think this dog is too thin, it is at the correct weight for its breed and performance event (lure coursing).

more than a quarter of an inch apart, the dog is overweight. (Note: Old dogs tend to carry most of their excess fat in the neck area; they may actually be thin in other areas.)

b) To check the ribs, stand with your dog beside you facing his rear. Place your thumb on the middle of his spine half way down the back, and spread your fingers out over his last few ribs. Run your fingers up and down along his ribcage. You should be able to feel the bumps of his ribs without pressing in.

c) To check the hips, run your hand over your dog's croup. You should be able to feel the bumps of his two pelvic bones without pressing down.

Some of you may be reading this and thinking, "I would never want my dog to be that skinny!" Think of Olympic athletes. If you want your dog to be an athlete, it is only fair that you help him achieve the body that he will need to perform and stay healthy and injury-free for many years (Fig. 4.10).

6. People worry that their dogs will not get enough nutrition if they feed less.

Premium dog foods are packed with nutrients. If your dog is overweight, unless he has a hormonal problem (e.g., hypothyroidism), he is getting too much nutrition, and reducing his intake will not put him in jeopardy. Remember: just like humans, individual dogs vary in their metabolic rate, and some dogs just need less food.

7. People don't know how to get their dogs to lose weight without all the side effects — begging, that sad-eyed look that says, "I'm hungry", etc.

Theoretically, it is a simple matter to cause a dog to lose weight — just feed less and/or exercise more. But, when dogs are fed less, they sometimes act as if they are hungry all of the time. So try the pumpkin diet. Reduce your dog's regular food by 25 to 33 percent, and replace it with twice as much canned pumpkin (not the kind with sugar and spices, ready-made for pies — you want just plain, pureed pumpkin). For example, if you are currently feeding your dog three cups of food (remember to include snacks and training tidbits in your total), you would instead feed him two cups of food and two cups of canned pumpkin. Dogs love the pumpkin — it has the texture of canned dog food, it provides vitamins and roughage, it makes them feel full (so they don't forage in the yard for leftovers), and they lose weight! Measure your dog's food in a measuring cup — don't guess at it. If your dog is fed just one percent more than he needs, by middle age he will be 25 percent overweight. When your dog has achieved a normal weight, the amount of food can be gradually increased and the pumpkin decreased until he maintains his weight, neither losing nor gaining. The final amount you feed should be less than the dog was fed when he was overweight.

8. The veterinarian said that the dog was a good weight (or even underweight).

I have asked many veterinarians why they don't tell their clients that their dogs are overweight, and I always get the same answer: "I have lost so many clients because they were offended when I told them their dogs were overweight that I just don't tell them anymore." So please, don't be offended — your dog's weight doesn't reflect on you personally.

Another benefit of weight loss is that your dog's required jump height may be lower. Reducing the weight of a Rottweiler from conformation weight to working weight can take more than an inch off the dog's height at the withers, and that may reduce his performance jump height. Fat does not contribute to performance. In addition to adding dead weight that increases the wear and tear on bones and joints, it places a strain on the cardiovascular system. Remember, every pound of fat contains a mile of capillaries.

Performance dogs should be weighed monthly and their weight recorded. A weight change can be the first sign of disease. You can weigh a small or medium-sized dog by stepping on a scale while holding the dog in your arms, then subtracting your weight from the total. Larger dogs are too heavy to lift easily, and the scale may not be able to measure the combined weight of owner and dog. However, most veterinarians will not charge you to weigh your dog on their professional scale. Another option for weighing large dogs is to purchase a postal scale and cover it with a board on which the dog can stand.

DIET

It can be virtually guaranteed that, in any group of ten dog owners, there will be ten people who insist that their way of feeding dogs is the best. Discussions of dog foods come second only to religion in terms of the fervor of their proponents. The fact is, there are many different balanced dog foods on the market, and several of them (but not necessarily all) will be suitable for a given dog. Knowledge of canine nutrition is important for owners who want to ensure that they are providing their dogs with a complete and balanced diet. But, unfortunately, in most discussions of canine nutrition, there is a certain amount of misinformation. Why? Because the dog food companies have done the vast majority of the research on canine nutrition, and they are under no obligation to completely inform the buying public of their findings. The data are locked away in company files and rarely published in refereed journals — those that have submitted manuscripts reviewed and accepted by at least two experts in the field.

Well, what do we know for sure? Most performance dogs should be fed premium quality dry dog foods made by companies that specialize in diets formulated for dogs with different activity levels and needs. Such dog foods are generally the result of controlled research and are complete and well-balanced. A dog food is complete if it contains all of the components (amino acids, fats, vitamins, minerals, etc.) required by a dog. It is balanced if those components are in the correct proportions. There are several classes of essential nutrients in the diet of dogs. The nutrient allowances of protein, fat, minerals, vitamins, and trace metals for dogs as recommended by the Association of American Feed Control Officials (AAFCO) are listed in Table 4.1. In addition, dogs should have fresh water available at all times. Dogs need 50 mL (2 ounces) of water per day for every pound of body weight. This means that a 70-pound dog drinks almost a gallon of water a day. The water should be changed daily, because stale water can contain bacteria and fungi.

A table of the caloric requirements of dogs of different body weights and activity levels is provided in Table 4.2. At the time of writing, most dog foods do not list caloric content on the label, but it is expected that more will do so in the future. Energy can be supplied by protein, fat, and carbohydrates. Carbohydrates are the most efficient source of energy. Complex carbohydrates like corn, wheat, and rice are a rapidly available source of energy. Fats also supply energy in addition to essential fatty acids and fat-soluble vitamins. Very high levels of

Table 4.1		
AAFCO Nutrient Profiles for Adult Maintenance Food		
Nutrient	*Min. Amount (dry wt.)*	*Units*
Protein	18	%
Fat	5	%
Minerals		
Calcium	0.6	%
Phosphorus	0.5	%
Ca:P Ratio	1:1	
Potassium	0.6	%
Sodium	0.06	%
Chloride	0.09	%
Magnesium	0.04	%
Iron	80	mg/kg
Copper	7.3	mg/kg
Manganese	5.0	mg/kg
Zinc	120	mg/kg
Iodine	1.5	mg/kg
Selenium	0.11	mg/kg
Vitamins		
Vitamin A	5000	IU/kg
Vitamin D	500	IU/kg
Vitamin E	50	IU/kg
Thiamin	1.0	mg/kg
Riboflavin	2.2	mg/kg
Pantothenic acid	10.0	mg/kg
Niacin	11.4	mg/kg
Pyridoxine	1.0	mg/kg
Folic acid	0.18	mg/kg
Vitamin B12	0.02	mg/kg
Choline	1200	mg/kg

Adapted from: Case LP, Carey DP. Hirakawa DA, *Canine and Feline Nutrition. A Resource for Companion Animal Professionals*, Mosby, St. Louis, 1995, Appendix 3, p.430.

fat are not necessary for most dogs. An exception is dogs, such as sled dogs, that are working hard every day or that live outdoors in cold weather. High levels of fat should be avoided in dogs that have had pancreatitis (inflammation of the pancreas). Proteins supply only a small amount of the energy used in exercise. Many of the premium quality dog foods, marketed for puppies and for active working dogs, contain very high levels of protein. There is no evidence that this much protein is beneficial to most dogs, or even that it is completely digested

Table 4.2
Caloric Requirements of Dogs

Body Weight (lb.)	House Dog (calories)	Active Dog (calories)	Working Dog (calories)
10	400	500	600
25	700	875	1050
50	1400	1750	2100
75	1800	2250	2700
100	2400	3000	3600
125	3000	3750	4500
150	3600	4500	5400

and utilized. A protein level of 22 to 25 percent is perfectly adequate for most performance dogs.

A major concern regarding protein is its availability to the dog. Feeding a high level of protein is useless if the food cannot be absorbed by the gastrointestinal tract or used by the body. Protein sources have widely varying digestibility. For example, eggs are highly digestible, whereas meat meal is less digestible. Further, a given source of protein, such as poultry by-product meal, may have poor to excellent digestibility, depending on the supplier. It is important to become familiar with the terminology on the dog food label and avoid dog foods that are comprised of protein derived from difficult to digest sources.

Federal law requires that dog food labels state the minimum amount of protein and fat and the maximum amount of fiber and moisture in the dog food. The label must also list all of the ingredients in the dog food, starting with the most abundant. There are many terms on these labels of which a buyer should be aware. "Offal" and "by-products" are two terms that refer to the parts of an animal which were left over after the meaty parts were removed for human consumption. Thus, chicken offal includes intestines, feet, and feathers. Although offal, strictly speaking, may contain a certain amount of protein, this protein is likely to be less readily digested by the dog and thus may not be available for the dog to use as nutrients. Table 4.3 lists what to look for on the dog food bag.

Be aware, however, that dog food companies frequently change the composition of their dog foods, so the label on a given dog food today may be

Table 4.3
Dog Food Labels

Item	Importance
Nutritional guarantee	Guarantees that the product is adequate for a specific life stage (growth, maintenance, etc.).
Validation of the nutritional guarantee	Indicates that the product has been tested in animal feeding tests using AAFCO procedures. This is important because there is no legal requirement for a dog food to have been tested in dogs.
Net weight	Helps you compare costs.
Ingredient panel	In decending order of abundance by wet weight. Everything must be listed, but there is no requirement for the manufacturer to state the quality of the ingredients.
Company information	There should be a name, address, 800 number, E-mail address, and Website so that you can contact the manufacturer.
Satisfaction guarantee	This should state exactly what to do if you are not satisfied and how the manufacturer will remedy the problem.
Expiration date	This should state the date by which the food should be fed, not the date on which it was manufactured.

different tomorrow. Therefore, it's best to save the label of your current bag of food and periodically check your new bags to be sure that you are buying a food with the same constituents in the same proportions. Another problem with dog food labeling is that the dog food companies are not required to list the availability of nutrients in any objective way. Therefore, it is your responsibility to observe your dog's activity level, temperament, coat, and weight for changes that might be associated with its food. A word of caution: although we are often told that the condition of a dog's coat is an indication of the dog's general health, this is not necessarily true. In the past, people fed arsenic to their dogs to improve their coats, and arsenic can kill!

Many dog breeders today do not recommend the use of puppy foods or high protein foods for performance dogs of any age. They recommend feeding premium adult maintenance diets to both puppies and active adults. Published research supports this premise. In one study, litters of Labrador Retriever puppies were divided into two groups: those that received a good quality food *ad lib* and were supplemented with vitamins and minerals, and those that were fed 75 percent of the amount that their littermates chose to eat and were not supplemented with vitamins or minerals. The dogs that were fed *ad lib* and supplemented had a higher incidence and severity of hip dysplasia and a number of other bone and joint abnormalities than their limit-fed littermates.

Calcium and phosphorus are the most important minerals in the diet of all dogs, and particularly growing puppies. Although the ratio of calcium to phosphorus in a dog food is important, recent studies suggest that the total amount of calcium ingested may be more important. Excess calcium is thought to contribute to the development of hip and elbow dysplasia, osteochondrosis dissecans and other bone and joint problems. At the time of writing, all premium adult maintenance dog foods produced by major manufacturers have enough calcium to support the healthy growth of puppies, even those of the giant breeds. Resist the urge to provide extra supplementation with vitamins and with minerals such as bone meal, as this may result in the feeding of excess calcium. In addition, there are several nutritional supplements on the market that contain high levels of calcium. These should be avoided.

The water soluble vitamins include vitamin C, thiamin, riboflavin, niacin, biotin, and pantothenic acid, names that you will find familiar from reading your cereal box in the morning. The daily requirements of all of these vitamins are supplied in premium dog food. It is generally thought that an excess of these water soluble vitamins is harmless, since they are readily secreted in the urine. However, it has been shown in humans that excessive quantities of niacin can produce diabetes, gout, and liver failure and can decrease the amount of energy that is supplied to the heart during exercise in the form of free fatty acids. In addition, there have been reports of an increased incidence of congenital brain malformations in puppies of bitches oversupplemented with vitamin B_{12}.

Unlike humans, dogs synthesize their own vitamin C on a continuous basis. Although the popular literature is filled with anecdotal reports of the benefits of vitamin C in reducing bone and joint problems such as hip dysplasia, there is no adequately controlled research to prove this. It is therefore difficult to be sure of any benefits to supplementing dogs' diets with vitamin C. Ultimately, this remains a decision for each individual to make. However, it is probably best not to supplement with megadoses of the vitamin. In humans, who need to take vitamin C in their diet, excess vitamin C has been associated with kidney stones. In addition it reduces the availability of vitamin B_{12} in food and causes bone and joint abnormalities when it is removed after having been given over a long period of time. This would suggest that excess vitamin C in dogs, which are capable of synthesizing their own, may also have serious consequences.

Because the fat-soluble vitamins A, D, E, and K are stored for months in the body, dogs can suffer toxic effects when given an excess of these vitamins. Oversupplementation of vitamin D can cause osteoporosis (thinning of the bones), and too much vitamin A can cause the bones to become abnormally thick, causing pressure on the spinal cord.

Only very small amounts of the trace metals (iron, chromium, and zinc) are needed in the diet. These can be found in meat and grains and are also provided as a supplement in premium dog foods. A balanced diet is still the best source of all of the vitamins and minerals required for optimum health. There are reports of individual cases of dogs fed premium dog foods that need supplementation with minerals, particularly zinc. These dogs may be unable to absorb the minerals from their food.

There is a tendency for premium foods to be low in fiber (often as low as four percent). This means that the diet is highly digestible, and causes a reduction in the size of the stools. However, if a particular food makes your dog constipated, it may have too little fiber for his digestive system.

Several years ago, there was a great deal of controversy over the use of ethoxyquin as a preservative in dog foods. Controlled studies in dogs have now shown an association between cancer in dogs and foods containing ethoxyquin. Thus, dog foods that contain this preservative should be avoided. Most premium dog foods now use natural preservatives such as vitamins C and E.

The following are basic guidelines for planning a performance dog's diet:
1. Use a complete, balanced, premium dry dog food.
2. Feed moderate levels of protein.
3. Adjust the fat levels according to your dog's activity level and metabolic rate.
4. Feed a quality puppy food until eight weeks of age, and then gradually switch to adult dog food by four months of age.

5. Do not give vitamin or mineral supplements to puppies.
6. Experiment as necessary. If your dog is not doing as well as you would like on one dog food, try another.

Remember, if you have more than one dog, it is not necessary, nor even a good idea to feed them all the same dog food. Each dog's needs should be assessed individually, and the dog fed appropriately. Don't hesitate to give your dog a little human food with his meal — cottage cheese, yogurt, and vegetables can add variety and roughage. It is probably best to feed dogs twice a day. Occasionally, dogs fed only once a day will vomit bile-containing fluid at the end of a 24-hour period, when their stomachs are completely empty. Some people recommend feeding a hyperactive dog twice a day, as it can tone down their energy level. However, many people find that, because of time constraints on the working person, it is better to give the dog just a snack, such as a large, nutritionally balanced dog biscuit, in the morning. Then they can use the rest of the morning time to get some exercise.

Finally, a word about hypoallergenic diets (often lamb and rice-based). These diets are just fine for dogs. However, I prefer not to feed them as the routine diet for my dogs, but to keep them in reserve in case my dog develops allergies and has to be put on a hypoallergenic diet. These lamb and rice diets are hypoallergenic precisely because so few dogs encounter lamb as a source of protein. (Perhaps these diets are not hypoallergenic to Australian dogs!) Hypoallergenic diets are designed to be used in dogs that have food allergies. Food allergies are much less common in dogs than inhalant allergies, those due to grasses, molds, and other inhaled allergens. However, some benefits have been noticed when hypoallergenic diets are fed to dogs with inhalant allergies, so it is probably worth experimenting with these diets for these dogs.

EXERCISE AND CONDITIONING

Every dog, and especially performance dogs, should be on a regular exercise program. Principles for the development of fitness programs for performance dogs are discussed in detail in Chapter 5.

WHEN TO SEE YOUR VETERINARIAN

You are your dog's first veterinarian — the first one to appreciate that your dog is not well. Because you know your dog intimately and observe him every day, you will be able to see subtle signs of illness that your veterinarian would not notice. Astute observation is definitely the key to detecting illness in a dog before it becomes serious. The following pages describe some of the common clinical signs of disease in dogs.

Change in Temperament

As most people have experienced, being ill can make you crabby. The same is true for some dogs. Other dogs internalize their pain or discomfort, and the only signs may be a tenseness in the facial muscles, a slight reduction in alertness, or tension in the back or abdominal muscles.

Change in Activity Level

Reduction in a dog's activity, or a lack of interest in normal household activities, may be one of the first signs that a dog is uncomfortable or feeling pain. This finding is not specific to any particular disease state and is found in animals that are ill for any one of a number of reasons.

Reduction in Food Intake

Another sign of illness is a change in dietary intake, usually a reduction of food consumption (anorexia). Anorexia may be complete or partial. In partial anorexia, a dog will appear to be interested in food and may pick at its dinner, but will not ingest adequate amounts of food. Dogs with complete anorexia show no interest in food whatsoever.

There are several reasons for a reduction in food intake. The most common reason is systemic disease (involving the whole body). Whenever there is a systemic illness, particularly involving fever, biochemical substances circulate in the blood and tell the brain that the animal is not hungry. Another example of a systemic disease that induces anorexia is cancer. People with cancer often report that their taste sensations have changed. They cannot taste sweets as well, so food tastes more bitter. Presumably this also happens to dogs. Another cause of anorexia is gastrointestinal disease. These disorders may include mouth pain due to bad teeth, gastritis (inflammation of the stomach lining), diarrhea, or constipation. Finally, anorexia may be neurologically induced. The brain has control centers that tell the dog when it is hungry and when it has had enough food. If there has been damage to the brain because of trauma, a tumor, or inflammation, these eating centers may malfunction and cause the dog to become anorexic. Even subtle changes in a dog's life, such as moving to a new house, being boarded, or the addition of new animals to the home, may cause enough stress to affect the eating center of the brain.

Change in Body Weight

If a change in dietary intake has lasted several days or more, it will result in a change in body weight. It is especially important to record the weight of your performance dog on a regular basis. Since weight gain or loss is controlled by the net effects of dietary intake and physical exercise, dogs that are expending a great deal of energy in performance events may lose weight rapidly in response to small reductions in dietary intake.

Poor Coat

The skin and coat mirror your dog's health. Illness almost always causes changes in the coat, such as dryness or hair loss. Although these changes may be subtle at first, if you are observant, you can detect small changes that indicate that your dog is not in peak physical condition. Have you ever noticed that your well-groomed, minimally shedding dog deposits hair and dander all over the veterinarian's office? That is due to the almost instantaneous effects of corticosteroids, the main hormone secreted during stress. When dogs are stressed or ill, the body releases corticosteroids internally to help the dog cope with stress. However, one of the side effects of steroids is that they cause the hair follicles to stop producing hair. If this happens over a period of time, it will be noticed as hair loss over and above the normal amount of shedding. Occasionally a dog will develop a hormonal imbalance in which very large amounts of endogenous steroids are released from the adrenal gland, and these dogs may become almost bald from extreme hair loss.

Vomiting

Dogs vomit readily because some of the muscles in their esophagus are under voluntary control. These muscles are a holdover from their ancestors, wolves, who eat large amounts at a kill and then travel to the den and vomit to provide food for their pups. If a dog feels a slightly upset stomach, it can consciously decide to vomit. This is why a dog can eat its dinner rapidly, and then, feeling too full, vomit the meal up, and proceed to eat it again. This seems disgusting to us but is routine to the dog. Therefore, a single occurrence of vomiting in a dog should be noted, but is not worthy of a trip to the veterinarian. Vomiting is serious if it occurs repeatedly, if the vomit contains blood, or if it is accompanied by other signs of illness. Nausea often precedes vomiting. Dogs that feel nauseated may hang their heads, salivate, and make repeated swallowing motions.

Diarrhea

Diarrhea is an increase in the water content of the stools and indicates that the intestine is not properly functioning. Many dogs suffer from occasional bouts of loose stools. This generally clears up within 24 hours and is not considered serious unless it persists or is accompanied by other signs of illness. Persistent or bloody diarrhea, especially with very watery stools, is definitely a cause for concern. If your dog has persistent diarrhea, you should provide your veterinarian with the following information: how long the dog has had diarrhea, whether there have been changes in the diet, the quantity, color, and consistency of the stool, the frequency of defecation, and whether the dog is straining when defecating. In addition, you should bring a fresh stool sample for the veterinarian to examine and test.

A dog with severe diarrhea can become dehydrated very rapidly. This is especially true of small dogs and puppies. Dehydration can significantly reduce the blood volume, causing a dog to go into shock and die. A dog suffering from dehydration is weak, and its eyes may look sunken. When the skin is pinched, it will not spring back but will remain in a tent for several seconds. A dehydrated dog should be administered intravenous fluids by a veterinarian immediately.

Fever

The normal temperature for a dog is 100.2 to 102.8°F (37.8 to 39.3°C). Large dogs tend to have normal temperatures at the lower end of this range and smaller dogs at the upper end. A dog's temperature may be measured by inserting a rectal thermometer (it helps if the end is lubricated) about three inches into the rectum and holding it there for one minute. For the most accurate measurement, the thermometer should be held against the wall of the rectum. Although an elevated temperature is often a sign that the dog's body is fighting an infection, internal body temperature can also be elevated by exercise and by stress. Fevers of 103 to 106°F may indicate an infection, especially if accompanied by other signs of systemic disease. Temperatures greater than 106°F are rare and usually indicate hyperthermia (heatstroke) rather than infection. Heatstroke is a life-threatening condition and requires immediate treatment by wrapping the dog in cold, wet towels as soon as possible and transporting to a veterinarian.

Increased Drinking and Urination

A normal dog should drink 50 mL (approximately 2 ounces) of water per pound of body weight and should produce 25 mL of urine per pound. There are many different causes of excessive water intake and urination. The most common cause is kidney disease. A damaged kidney cannot reabsorb enough of the fluid from the blood which it is filtering, and the fluid is instead lost in the urine. The water loss induces thirst, so the dog drinks more water. There are other, less common causes of excessive drinking and urination, such as diabetes, excessive adrenal hormone production, and some infections.

Some dogs just like to drink water, perhaps to relieve boredom, and as a result, they urinate excessively. One of my dogs will begin to drink water as soon as I return home from work. If I don't stop him, he may consume well over a gallon of water in less than 30 minutes. Within another half hour, he begins to look very distressed because he needs to go outside. If I still don't notice (I am sure he considers me dense at times), he will have an accident in the house and will produce floods of urine, mostly composed of water. Repeated tests of kidney function have failed to reveal a problem. This vice, which is called psychogenic polydypsia (*psycho* = in the mind; *genic* = origin; *poly* = repeated; *dypsia* = drinking) is relatively common in large dogs. Any dog that is drinking and urinating excessively over a period of time should be evaluated by a veterinarian.

Lameness
Lameness is caused by a reluctance on the dog's part to bear weight on the limb because of pain. Lameness is a significant problem in performance dogs and will be discussed in detail in Chapter 6.

HOW TO CHOOSE A VETERINARIAN
The criteria you should use to select a veterinarian are similar to those you would use to choose a personal physician. First, you should choose a veterinarian who is a good diagnostician and surgeon. Personal references from friends and acquaintances are of great help in making your selection. You can learn a great deal about local veterinarians by learning how they have handled illnesses in other people's dogs. Ask your friends and acquaintances if their veterinarians were able to make a diagnosis in most cases and the outcome of surgical procedures.

Your veterinarian must be a good communicator. She should be able and willing to answer your questions and should be able to explain, in terms you understand, the diagnosis and her recommendations for treatment and follow-up care. If your veterinarian doesn't know the diagnosis or the answers to your questions, she should at least be able to offer you an explanation of her thought processes and plans for further evaluation. Your veterinarian should be willing to listen to you and should not ignore your own observations of the dog's health status.

Your veterinarian should have a modern, AAHA-approved facility with capable veterinary assistants and access to a diagnostic lab that can give results of most tests within 24 hours. She should have staff on the premises 24 hours a day to care for seriously ill dogs or should be able to move seriously ill dogs to a 24-hour emergency facility for overnight care and observation. Your veterinarian should be available during emergency hours or should be able to refer you to an emergency clinic for problems that occur at night or on weekends.

Your veterinarian should be willing to refer your dog to a specialist for further evaluation and should not be threatened if you ask for a second opinion on the diagnosis. She should also be familiar with the requirements of the performance event(s) in which you participate, or if not, should be willing to learn.

You should *not* choose a veterinarian on the basis of the prices charged for services. A veterinarian has a great deal of time and money invested in her education and clinic. A veterinary clinic has a very high overhead because of the cost of maintaining all of the same equipment which is in a human hospital (surgical and anesthetic equipment, X-ray machine, ultrasound equipment, etc.) and personnel to care for your dog and assist with surgery. A veterinarian who is consistently charging less for her services than other local colleagues is probably cutting corners somehow, perhaps in a way that could affect your dog's care. To get the best care for your performance dog, you should expect to pay for it.

THE ANNUAL VETERINARY EXAMINATION

I cannot emphasize enough the importance of obtaining a thorough veterinary checkup on performance dogs once a year. Even though your dog may seem to be the picture of health, a veterinarian can often detect early signs of disease or organ malfunction before the dog shows any outward signs of problems, allowing you to treat the condition early or institute measures to prevent the condition from becoming worse. When you take your dog to the veterinarian, you should bring your records and a fresh stool sample with you. A veterinary assistant will check the sample for gastrointestinal parasites and will report to you the findings while you are there so that, if necessary, treatment can be instituted. A thorough veterinary examination should contain the components listed below.

History

The veterinarian should ask you questions regarding your observations of the dog's overall health. This is your opportunity to express any concerns you may have with respect to your dog's health or behavior. You may wish to point out any skin lumps you have found, or you may discuss changes in your dog's food or water intake or urination or bowel habits. If a specific problem has prompted your visit, you may wish to bring with you a written history of the problem. For example, if the dog has been vomiting periodically, try to have a written record of the date when the vomiting first began, how often the dog vomited, and the amount, color, and texture of the vomit.

Physical Examination

Your veterinarian has been trained to perform a detailed physical examination on your dog. As the veterinarian performs the examination, she is thinking about all of the dog's body systems and trying to determine whether they are functioning at their peak. The veterinarian should look in the dog's mouth, eyes, and ears, and should run her hands over the dog's body, examining all parts and feeling for swellings or abnormalities in the size or shape of lymph nodes under the skin and of abdominal organs. The veterinarian should listen to the heart and the lungs with a stethoscope, take the dog's temperature, and weigh the dog.

Heartworm Check

Heartworms are parasites that live in the hearts of dogs, eventually causing heart failure. They are transmitted by mosquitoes. Heartworm disease exists in most areas of the United States and in southern Canada. In some areas, the infection rate of heartworm in dogs not receiving heartworm preventive is over 50 percent. Treatment of the adult worms in the heart is difficult. It requires intensive care of the dog and can be life-threatening. Therefore, the key to controlling heartworm infestation lies in preventing the adult worms from ever becoming established in the heart. Several excellent products are available for preventing heartworm infection in dogs. But before a dog is placed on heartworm preventive, a blood sample must be tested to ensure that it is not harboring adult worms in the heart. This can be done in the veterinarian's office while you wait. In northern areas, dogs need to be on heartworm preventive only during the warmer months. These dogs should get a heartworm test in the spring, before being placed on preventive medication. In the south, however, mosquitoes may be present year-round, and it is recommended that dogs that live in or visit the South be given heartworm preventive throughout the year. These dogs should still be tested every year, just in case the medication was forgotten or for some reason was ineffective. Heartworm preventive can be given to a puppy with its first set of vaccinations. In a puppy that young, a heartworm test is not necessary.

Vaccinations

During the health checkup, the veterinarian will give your dog its annual vaccinations. The vaccinations are given to provide immunity to a variety of infectious diseases that a dog may encounter. The infectious agents for which vaccinations are available are listed in Table 4.4. Performance dogs, because they tend to come in contact with many dogs from a variety of sources at performance events, should be given a complete panel of vaccinations, and these should be kept up to date, according to your veterinarian's instructions. Most vaccinations are given once a year with the exception of the rabies vaccine, which are given every one to three years, depending on the region. Some veterinarians recommend administering vaccinations for parvovirus and coronavirus semiannually, because of the increased likelihood of exposure to these organisms at performance events.

I frequently hear of owners of performance dogs who administer vaccinations to their own dogs. I strongly caution against this. New vaccine formulations regularly become available, and most owners don't have the medical background or the access to medical research that would allow them to make appropriate decisions on which vaccinations to administer. In addition, dogs vaccinated by their owners may not get regular veterinary examinations.

Table 4.4
Diseases for Which Vaccinations Are Available

Agent/Disease	Clinical Signs
Rabies	Fatal neurological disease that can be transmitted to humans.
Distemper	Diarrhea, pneumonia, neurological disease
Infectious canine hepatitis	Diarrhea, pneumonia, depression
Parvovirus	Bloody diarrhea, dehydration
Coronavirus	Diarrhea
Kennel cough	Cough, pneumonia
Lyme disease	Lameness, arthritis, depression
Leptospirosis	Bloody urine, diarrhea, vomiting

Blood Chemistry and Urinalysis

If the veterinarian notices anything abnormal, she may take a blood sample and a urine sample to perform biochemical tests to detect infections and malfunctions of the liver, kidney, pancreas, muscle, thyroid, and other organ systems.

Take advantage of your appointments with your veterinarian. Ask questions, be sure you understand the answers, and use them as an opportunity to tune up your dog physically. Make your veterinarian a part of your performance team.

Suggested Reading:

Case LP, Carey DP, Hirakawa DA. *Canine and Feline Nutrition. A Resource for Companion Animal Professionals*. Mosby, St. Louis, 1995.

Cargill J, Thorpe-Vargas S. *Feed That Dog! A Complete Guide to Dog Nutrition*. Dog World Magazine. For reprints, call (800) 247-8080.

Two friends getting some winter exercise.

Marcia Halliday

5.

CONDITIONING THE

PERFORMANCE DOG

I own two dogs, and they both have been trained to respond immediately to my voice. For example, when we're outside, all I have to do is issue the following standard dog command: 'Here Earnest! Here Zippy! C'mon! Here! I said come HERE! You dogs COME HERE RIGHT NOW! ARE YOU DOGS LISTENING TO ME? HEY!!!' And instantly both dogs, in unison, like a precision drill team, will continue trotting in random directions, sniffing the ground.

Dave Barry

The key to all performance is the contraction of muscle tissue. Muscle provides the leverage that moves the bones. In order for muscles to contract, they must receive electrical stimuli from the nerves, and they must be provided with energy. Energy is supplied to the muscles in the form of oxygen and other nutrients via the blood stream. The cardiovascular system cannot provide oxygen to the muscles without adequate functioning of the lungs. Thus, the cardiovascular, respiratory, musculoskeletal, and nervous systems are all linked in the execution of athletic skills. If one of the links is weakened, performance suffers. The purpose of conditioning is to maximize the functioning of each of these body systems.

BENEFITS OF CONDITIONING

There is no doubt that canine performance is improving every year. Dogs in obedience are quicker and more precise, field trial dogs are retrieving at greater distances and in tougher conditions, flyball dogs are faster, and sled dogs are able to traverse greater distances in shorter times. There are many reasons for this continuous improvement in performance. One is that the population of dogs has grown rapidly over the last two decades (Fig. 5.1). This has provided a larger population from which to select dogs for performance events and has increased the size of the gene pool for performance dogs. In addition, there are more participants in canine performance events than ever; this stimulates competition and a greater exchange of ideas. Improved economic conditions allow people to invest in better training, both for themselves and their dogs, and to provide better training facilities and the leisure time in which to train. Finally, improvements in the quality of nutrition and of medical care for dogs in the last 25 years have also contributed greatly to improved performance.

Exercise and physical conditioning are of utmost importance to the performance dog. It is not enough, and indeed it is not fair, to provide a performance dog only with training towards the specific goals of the performance activity without also providing it with the opportunity to become physically fit in a broader sense. There are many physical and psychological benefits of fitness in addition to improving the dog's skills for a particular performance event. A regular program of exercise increases a dog's strength and coordination. This helps the dog perform better and reduces the likelihood of injuries. In addition, should an accident occur, a fit dog will be more likely to at least partially control his fall or soften his landing, thus reducing the likelihood of a severe injury.

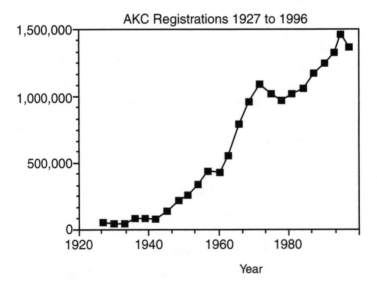

Fig. 5.1. There has been a steady increase in the number of dogs registered by the American Kennel Club from 1927 to the present. (Statistics courtesy of the American Kennel Club Library).

Exercise is an excellent way to control a dog's weight. Strong muscles are larger and utilize more calories while at rest than smaller, weaker muscles. Runners and other fitness buffs have long recognized the psychological benefits of exercise. Exercise causes endorphins to be released in the brain. Endorphins are neurotransmitters (biochemical messengers within the brain), some of which cause a feeling of euphoria and overall well-being. This can prevent a dog from developing harmful behaviors such as lick granulomas (caused by repeated licking or chewing at the skin, usually of the legs), destructive behavior (such as chewing the oriental rugs or digging up the tulip bulbs), restlessness, or excessive barking. Finally, dogs that participate in a program of regular exercise derive many physiological benefits. The respiratory and cardiovascular systems adapt and expand their capacities, enabling the dog to more readily oxygenate its blood and allowing more blood to be pumped to the muscles and other organs.

ORGANIZING A FITNESS PROGRAM

Before you start your dog on a fitness program, you should objectively evaluate his structure and current state of fitness and health. Is your dog ectomorphic, mesomorphic, or endomorphic? Does he have appropriate front and rear angulation for his breed? Does he have any structural faults that you should be aware of when designing a conditioning program? After all, the purpose of conditioning is to tune up his musculoskeletal system, not to break it down by overuse. You may benefit from obtaining an objective evaluation of your dog's structure by a breeder, judge, or other person knowledgeable about dogs in general and your breed in particular.

Objectively evaluate your dog's current level of fitness. Your dog is fit if it does not have any excess fat and has good muscle size and tone. Use the tips described in Chapter 4 to determine whether your dog has any excess subcutaneous fat. Evaluate your dog's muscle size and tone. Feel the muscles of the upper leg, the muscles of the shoulders and upper arms, and the muscles along the spine from the neck across the back and along the croup. Muscle size is partly genetic (endomorphic dogs tend to have greater muscle size than ectomorphs) and partly a reflection of the amount of exercise your dog has had longterm. Muscle size also changes with age. Puppies and older dogs have smaller muscles than dogs in their prime. Muscle tone is an indication of how much exercise your dog has had in the past few weeks. Toned-up muscles should feel firm, with indentations between muscle bundles. Compare the muscle size and tone of the muscles on the left and right sides of the body. If you feel asymmetry, it means that the dog has been using the muscles on one side more than the other. This could indicate that your dog is exercising preferentially on one side of the body, but more often it means that the dog is favoring the side with the smaller, less toned muscles. This happens when the dog feels weak or sore on one leg, such as with hip dysplasia. Although this condition affects both hips, one is usually more sore than the other at any given time. Finally, make sure that your dog has had its annual veterinary checkup and has been evaluated for hereditary conditions that can affect performance or that could be adversely affected by exercise. The most common of these conditions are hip dysplasia, elbow dysplasia, cataracts, and other ocular conditions that affect vision, cardio-vascular disorders, and von Willebrand's disease (a bleeding disorder). Indi-vidual breeds have other conditions that can affect performance. Many of the conditions that affect performance are discussed in Chapters 6 and 7.

If your dog has a condition that could affect performance or that could be adversely affected by exercise, consult with a veterinarian familiar with your performance events to determine the degree to which your dog can participate. Remember, you are your dog's coach. If your dog has hip dysplasia or another condition that results in arthritis, it is essential that your dog get enough exercise on a daily basis to strengthen the muscles that support the joints. On the other hand, it is important not to exercise your dog so much that you cause excess wear and tear on the joints of the rear legs. Learn to identify the earliest signs that your dog is tiring, and stop then, not when he is exhausted.

WARM-UPS AND COOL-DOWNS

Whenever training or competing with your dog, you should always begin with warm-up exercises. A warm-up dilates the blood vessels, increasing the supply of oxygen and nutrients to the muscles and nerves. It helps stretch the muscles, ligaments, and tendons. It aligns the bones and distributes joint fluid over the surfaces of the joints. In studies in humans, 70 percent of people who exercised without a warm-up developed abnormalities in the electrical signals to their hearts. In a study of Olympic athletes running the 100-meter race, those who did not warm up ran seven percent slower. This is the difference between winning and finishing dead last. Comparison studies of racing greyhounds in the United States and Australia have shown that the dogs in the United States more frequently suffer injuries such as pulled muscles and torn tendons during races. These studies show that more injuries result when warm-ups are omitted; dogs in the United States are not permitted to be warmed up prior to the race.

The following is a set of warm-up exercises that takes only 90 seconds to perform. A good start to the warm-up is to give your dog a quick rubdown, to make him aware of all of the parts of his body. Stand facing the same direction as your dog (who is also standing), and move your thumbs from the midline of the dog outward about 2 to 3 inches. Work your way from the nose all the way to the tail. Next, place your thumb and index finger on each side of the tail and run them down the length of the tail. Then use your palms to rub down the sides of your dog's face, down the front of the chest and the front legs, down the sides of the legs, down the sides of the chest and abdomen, and then down the front and back of the rear legs. Finally, pick up each one of your dog's feet and separate the toes gently so that the dog is made aware of each of them.

Next, have your dog stretch and flex his spine. Dogs love to stretch, especially when they first get up. You can train your dog to stretch on command by naming the behavior when it naturally occurs. Give a command such as "Stretch" when your dog stretches on his own. Your dog will soon make the association and stretch on command. Next, have your dog flex his spine from side to side. You can have the dog bend around your leg by holding his flank to your leg and then using food to lure his head around to the base of his tail. Have your dog do a few quick spins to the right and the left. Be sure that he turns in both directions since he may prefer one over another. Then have him trot up and down for about 50 feet to loosen up and get his blood flowing. Finally, have the dog focus on you. When competing, you should arrive at this point just before entering the ring. This is just one suggested warm-up protocol. If you design your own, be sure to include exercises to flex and extend your dog's spine and legs, increase heart rate and blood flow, and finish up with focusing exercises.

A cool-down period after exercise is also important. If vigorous exercise is stopped suddenly, blood may pool in the extremities. During vigorous exercise, vessels have opened up to allow maximal circulation in the muscles. After exercise, the heart slows so it doesn't remove the blood from the tissues as well. This can make the dog dizzy. In addition, a cool-down period has an important psychological effect. Many people walk out of the ring with their dogs and immediately put them in their crates. They may be doing this to preserve the dog's energy for further competition that day, but it is extremely depressing for the dog to be working with you one moment and then be in seclusion the next. It is far better for your dog's psychological and physiological state to take a slow walk for about five minutes. Plan to use this time to tell him what a great dog he is and how proud you are of him — no matter what the result of the competition.

DESIGNING A CONDITIONING PROGRAM

A fitness program is a planned schedule of exercises tailored to an individual dog's needs. You, as your dog's coach and trainer, must construct a

Fig. 5.2. Skill training.

program to suit your particular dog. Conditioning includes skill training exercises (Fig. 5.2), strength training exercises, and endurance exercises. The needs of each dog are different and are dependent on such factors as the age of the dog, body type, current level of fitness, energy level, the chosen performance event(s), and concurrent medical or physical conditions.

Everyone with a performance dog practices skill training: training in the specific skills that are required in competition. But for a surprising number of dogs, their conditioning program contains no specific strength or endurance training exercises. Strength is important for events that require quick responsiveness, because adequate strength is required to overcome inertia and move the body in the desired direction. Strength is also required for rapid acceleration and for speed while running and jumping. Muscular strength also helps to prevent injury and increase joint stability. Endurance training helps a dog to perform longterm. It is particularly important for dogs that participate in events that require long distance running or other sustained activity, such as herding trials or field trials.

Conditioning and exercise modify the two different types of muscle fibers: fast-twitch and slow-twitch fibers. The main difference between these fibers is that they use different biochemical mechanisms to convert glucose into energy for muscle contraction. Strength training develops the fast-twitch muscle fibers, whereas endurance training strengthens the slow-twitch fibers. In people, the relative number of fast- and slow-twitch fibers is genetically determined. Thus, hereditary factors influence athletic success. Ectomorphic individuals tend to have more slow-twitch fibers, and therefore excel in athletic events requiring endurance. Endomorphs, who have more fast-twitch fibers, excel in events requiring strength. A comparable study has not been done in dogs, but if differences in muscle fibers exist among different breeds, it may explain in part why some breeds seem to have a natural aptitude for certain performance events.

Intensity, duration, and frequency of training must be considered when designing a conditioning schedule. Intensity is the degree of effort (both mental and physical) involved in an exercise. Thus, in obedience, heads-up heeling is an intense exercise, whereas the *Stand for Exam* exercise is not — unless the dog is fearful of strangers. Each dog has its own needs with respect to the intensity of training. Few dogs work best when trained in a continuous, intense fashion. Most need frequent breaks. A dog in the early stages of a training program or one who is learning a new and difficult exercise should have more frequent breaks for play or relaxation. As your dog becomes accustomed to the routine, he may be able to accept a greater amount of intensive training, but you should always be aware of the signs that he is growing bored or fatigued. Some of these signs include lying down, panting, yawning, and a general lack of enthusiasm and energy.

The duration of the training session should be inversely proportional to the intensity. A really intense training session should be short, while a low-key session or one with lots of breaks may be longer.

The frequency of training sessions may be dependent on several factors. First, if the dog is not preparing for competition or actively competing, fewer skill-training sessions a week may be required. Dogs that are actively competing may need more frequent practice. Some dogs never require and others do not respond well to frequent skill-training sessions. Such dogs should nevertheless be provided with frequent, regular conditioning exercises to maintain strength and endurance.

Fig. 5.3. A break for play.

Like human athletes, dogs benefit from variation in the intensity, frequency, and duration of training sessions. One way to provide variation is by interval training, in which the intensity of training is varied. This permits a much greater volume of training with less stress and less risk of staleness. For example, an obedience trainer may want to perfect a dog's precision in heeling, an activity that takes a great deal of concentration and can be stressful for the dog. Most dogs benefit more from multiple short sessions of intense, concentrated heeling interspersed with exercises requiring less physical accuracy and concentration (i.e., interval training) than from a long, continuous session of heeling. In addition, dogs learn more rapidly and retain their lessons better if the training load is divided into specific, planned cycles.

Human athletes who train intensively for long periods of time can suffer from a psychological and physiological syndrome called staleness. The athlete begins to enjoy training less, feels tired, and may have difficulty eating, sleeping, and in personal relationships. A similar phenomenon has been observed in dogs that are trained intensively day after day, week after week. Experienced dog trainers can usually recognize some of the signs of staleness in a dog, but beginning trainers often may not. These dogs may suffer severe setbacks both in performance and attitude. The treatment for staleness is to give the dog a significant break from training and competition and to resume training gradually and with frequent breaks for play (Fig. 5.3). The best way to prevent staleness is

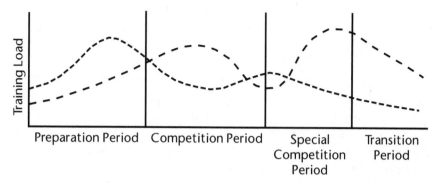

Preparation Period Competition Period Special Competition Period Transition Period

Fig. 5.4. Graph demonstrating the relationship between intensity (- - - - -) and volume (— — —) of training in preparation for a season of competitions. The volume of training increases first, followed by the intensity. During the competitive season, volume and intensity are inversely related. (Adapted from A.C. Fisher and C.R. Jensen. *Scientific Basis of Athletic Conditioning.* Philadelphia: Lea & Febiger, 1990.)

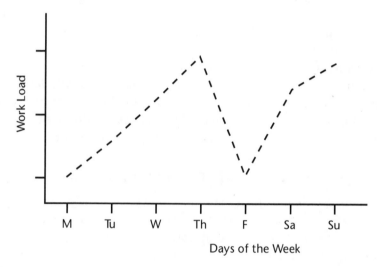

Days of the Week

Fig. 5.5. Graph illustrating changes in work load (both volume and intensity) during a weekly training cycle. (Adapted from Fisher and Jensen, *Scientific Basis of Athletic Conditioning.*)

to provide variety in the intensity, duration, and frequency of training, and to provide the dog with periodic long breaks and lots of play while training.

Training sessions should increase in duration and intensity gradually to allow the dog to be at peak skill level, strength, and endurance during the competition season (Fig. 5.4). If the competitive season is followed by a special competition (for example, a national competition held after the fall trial season), the special competition should be preceded by a period of reduced volume (the combination of frequency and duration) and intensity and then another increase in training volume.

Most canine athletic events have weekend competitions. Training requires significant forethought to keep the dog's performance at its peak and avoid staleness throughout several months of weekend showing. Immediately prior to the competition, the intensity of training should be reduced, a procedure called tapering. Tapering allows the athlete to have maximal performance without becoming stressed. A dog that is being prepared for weekend shows may be worked lightly on Monday and then trained with increasing intensity until Thursday. It may be given Friday off or may be provided with a fun, relaxed workout, emphasizing easy skills rather than intensity or endurance and given many breaks for play (Fig. 5.5). Such a cycle permits the dog to increase its skills and strength over a long season without becoming stale. There are several ways to introduce variation to a conditioning program: choosing different exercises, performing the exercises in a different order, or varying the number and length of training and rest/play periods.

Crosstraining should also be a component of your conditioning program. A dog that is trained exclusively for one performance event will develop muscles that help it to perform that event, but other muscle groups that are used less will be weaker. Dogs that are trained to participate in several different performance events will have better overall strength and coordination for a variety of tasks.

EXERCISES FOR STRENGTH AND ENDURANCE

Strength training exercises are those in which the dog moves an object (usually its weight) over a short distance. Thus, retrieving, in which the dog first accelerates, then slows, picks up the object, and accelerates again to return, is a strength training exercise. Other strength training exercises include dogs wrestling, jumping, chasing, and being chased. Endurance exercises are those in which the dog performs repeated motions at a relatively continuous speed, for 20 minutes or more on land, or for 10 minutes or more on water. Thus, roadwork (having the dog trot while you run, inline skate, bicycle, or otherwise keep up with it) is an endurance exercise. Swimming is an endurance exercise if the dog swims continuously for 10 minutes. On the other hand, if the dog is going in and out of the water for short retrieves, that is a strength-training exercise.

A successful program of physical fitness should have several characteristics. It should contain more than one exercise so that different groups of muscles are worked and the dog's interest maintained. It should start off gently and progress towards an achievable goal, so that a certain level of strength and endurance is developed and so that the dog experiences success. Finally, it should contain activities that are enjoyable to both dog and owner.

If a dog participates in performance events only seasonally, the exercise program should be modified accordingly. During the off season, the dog should be fed less and should be given moderate exercise (at least 15 minutes a day). This might consist of intense play with other dogs, a game of fetch (you can hit a tennis ball with a racket to increase its distance), or a run with you. One of the most enjoyable ways to give your dog moderate exercise is to take it for a walk. Most dogs love to go for walks because of their natural curiosity about the environment. They love to be surrounded by new sights and smells. It is best if the dog is trained to trot at a continuous speed, rather than walk or pace, and not permitted to stop at every post and fire hydrant. If you have a large dog, you may not be able to keep up when the dog is moving at a fast trot, but you can teach him to jog. Begin by starting off running with your dog at a fast trot (you may be able to go only a few hundred feet at first). Gradually slow your dog down while keeping him in a trot. The key is to stop before your dog changes gait to a pace or a walk. After a few weeks, your dog will jog on command at a speed you can keep up with.

It's best to have your dog walk out in front of you, rather than beside you, so that your dog's spine doesn't bend as he turns to look at you. It may also be helpful to use a body lead or other mechanism to attach the dog to your waist, thus leaving your hands free to swing as you walk. When starting, use sidewalks as a guide to keep your dog walking straight. When training my dogs to walk in this way, I carry a light stick to tap on the dog's flank if it begins to lag. I give the command "Let's go!" for the dog to trot out straight ahead of me and to put some tension on the lead. When we get to a crossroad, this same command means that we are going to continue across the road. I use the command, "This way," accompanied by a tug on the lead to the right or left, to signify to the dog that we are going to make a turn. The command, "Move over," means to shift to the left to allow a car to go by, because on roads with no sidewalks, we walk facing traffic. (Note: dogs and handlers walking at night should wear a harness or vest with reflective tape.) A jog of 20 minutes or more is an excellent endurance exercise. For owners who like to jog or run, the company of a dog can reduce boredom and provide a more intensive cardiovascular workout for the dog than a walk can afford.

About eight weeks before the competition season begins, your exercise program should escalate gradually to at least 30 minutes a day, and your dog's

Fig. 5.6. A Springer® can be used to exercise one or more dogs at a fast trot.

Fig. 5.7. These dogs are harnessed to their owner's bicycle by a retractable leash. They pull her on the bike several miles a day, a good endurance exercise.

dietary intake should increase accordingly. More strenuous endurance exercise usually involves roadwork in which the dog trots quickly. Bicycling with a loose dog is dangerous. Even on country paths, a loose dog can chase wild animals such as rabbits or deer and become lost or injured. But holding onto a dog's leash while bicycling can also be dangerous because your hands are needed for steering and braking. There are at least two products on the market by which a dog can be connected to a bicycle using a harness to leave the cyclist's hands free. One is the Springer®, a device that attaches to the dog by a nonrestrictive harness (one which does not impede the movement of the dog's front legs) to the bicycle frame at a stable location below the seat. The device has a strong spring that permits the dog a considerable range of movement, and it has a quick release that will free the dog in case it should run on the wrong side of an immovable object such as a lamp post. The Springer® can help you provide enough endurance training for a medium to large dog (Fig. 5.6). Another device is called the K9 Cruiser®. This mechanism attaches the dog to a bar connected to the bicycle's rear axle. One person I know has designed a system to attach her dogs' harnesses to the bars of her bicycle by a retractable leash (Fig. 5.7).

Mechanized treadmills are another way to provide roadwork, and they can be quite useful when you can't get outside because of bad weather or illness, but they do have disadvantages. They are expensive, require a large amount of room indoors, and can be quite boring for the dog. In addition, some people feel that treadmills do not allow free, natural movement.

One of the best types of exercise for dogs is swimming. Because swimming is a non weight-bearing activity, it strengthens the cardiovascular and muscular systems without placing stress on bones and joints. This is especially helpful for dogs with degenerative joint disease. There are several ways you can exercise your dog through swimming. If you have access to a swimming pool, you can have your dog swim around the edge while you walk alongside. He may need to be on leash initially, and you can encourage him by dropping dog biscuits in the water ahead of him (most float). Be sure your dog swims in both directions around the pool so that he exercises his muscles evenly.

You can also put your dog in a nonrestrictive harness, such as a nylon tracking or sledding harness (Fig. 5.8) which is then attached to a stationary object on one side of the pool, leaving about 6 feet of rope attached to the dog. You can get in the pool and tread water in front of the dog, urging him to swim forward, and thus maintain tension on the rope. Periodically approach and pet your dog so that he has the feeling that he has caught up. This technique can be used in a pool as short as 12 feet across.

Fig. 5.8. This is a non-restrictive harness, one that allows the front legs freedom of movement.

Fig. 5.9. Swimming provides an excellent, non-weight-bearing exercise.

Another option is to take your dog to a safe pond to swim. Scout the area for broken glass, fishing line, and other hazards. Most retrievers (and many other breeds) can be easily induced to jump in the water by throwing a bumper or other object for them to retrieve (Fig. 5.9). If your dog does not love to retrieve, you can encourage him to swim with you, or sit in a rowboat or plastic dingy and call him as you row slowly around. Throw an occasional biscuit in the water if necessary (remember Hansel and Gretel, who dropped breadcrumbs as they walked so they could find their way back home). One of my Golden Retrievers devised the ideal way to exercise by swimming. Some friends had a pond with about ten ducks on it. The ducks were very savvy and knew well the ways of dogs. My dog, Cajun, would jump in and swim towards them, but they would always keep just a few feet ahead of him. As they approached the other end of the pond, the ducks would take off and fly casually back over Cajun's head, and Cajun would turn and continue the pursuit back across the pond. This procedure would be repeated endlessly until I commanded him to leave the pond. As we turned to leave, I could always hear the ducks chuckling . . .

Other methods of exercise can be used to strengthen certain groups of muscles or to add variety to an exercise program. Mushing, skijoring (in which a dog pulls a person over the snow on skis), and weight-pulling are good ways to strengthen a dog's rear legs. These activities are very strenuous and the dog should be carefully trained and the weights built up gradually. In addition, these activities should be limited to dogs over 14 months of age. Another fun winter exercise is to have your dog accompany you while cross-country skiing. Like skijoring, this provides the dog with a great deal of exercise in a short period of time because of the difficulty of walking or running in deep snow. In some dogs, snowballs form between the toes. This problem can be reduced by trimming excess hair from the bottom of the feet and by applying Vaseline® or Pam® spray liberally to the skin between the toes before going outside. An excellent alternative is to have the dog wear booties.

Another exercise to strengthen the rear legs is to have the dog retrieve an object by running uphill. This increases the amount of weight borne on the rear legs, thus increasing the amount of work the leg muscles perform. It is not advisable to use stairs to strengthen the rear legs, since most dogs are uncomfortable going down stairs, because their hocks tend to hit the backs of the steps.

Agility obstacles can be used to develop the strength of specific muscle groups and to improve coordination. The A-frame strengthens a dog's rear legs and feet. The dog walk improves a dog's ability to sense the location of and control its rear legs (Fig. 5.10). The teeter-totter improves a dog's sense of balance and coordination, because it forces the dog to utilize its center of gravity to tip the board before descending. The weave poles improve a dog's coordination and balance, and strengthen the muscles of the neck and back (Fig. 5.11).

Fig. 5.10. The agility dog walk improves a dog's ability to control its rear legs.

Fig. 5.11. The weave poles improve a dog's coordination and flexibility and strengthen the muscles of the neck and back.

Stationary exercises can be designed to strengthen specific muscles in a dog's body. For example, teaching a dog to sit up (beg) strengthens the muscles of the spine and abdomen. It generally takes a dog about a week (five minutes practice per day) to learn to sit up, because the muscles are strengthening during this time. A dog can also be taught to walk on its rear legs. This improves balance and further strengthens the muscles of the back, abdomen, and rear legs. When a dog knows how to sit up, it can be taught to go from that position into a stand and eventually back into a sitting up position again. This exercise greatly strengthens the muscles of the rear legs. There are many other stationary exercises which can be devised by an inventive coach or anyone who enjoys teaching a dog tricks.

CONDITIONING DOGS WITH PHYSICAL PROBLEMS

Moderation is the key to conditioning a dog with a physical condition such as hip dysplasia or patellar luxation, which can result in secondary degenerative joint disease. The amount of training should be modified in accordance with the severity of the condition. Degenerative joint disease can become more severe with increased use of the joints. In addition, excessive exercise can produce fatigue which increases the laxity (looseness) of the joints, causing further wear and tear and increasing the chance of injury.

Always be conscious of signs of fatigue in your dog. It is not enough to think that your dog will restrict its activity when it becomes tired, because many dogs will literally work until they drop, either because they have been commanded to do so or because they enjoy the work so much. Signs of fatigue include stumbling, an anxious look, excessive panting, and widening of the end of the tongue.

Excessive water intake should be avoided just before and immediately after exercise. Hard working dogs may drink a little water immediately before and during strenuous exercise. Right after the cooling off period, your dog should be given a moderate amount of cool water and allowed to rest quietly. Mushers have found that giving white rice to their dogs right after a run helps to replenish the glycogen (stored energy) in the muscles.

CONDITIONING PUPPIES

It is important for the growth and development of puppies that they have proper exercise. Puppies that are prevented from exercising do not grow as large and are not as physically developed and coordinated as those provided with adequate exercise. An exercise program for a puppy should not, however, include strenuous exercises such as roadwork or full-height jumping. The growth plates, soft areas of the bone from which bone growth occurs, do not close or harden until the puppy is about 14 months of age. Because these areas are soft, they are susceptible to injury. Injuries to the growth plates may result in reduced or uneven bone growth, leading to bone deformities. Puppies also have an increased risk of injury due to their relative lack of coordination, because their bones are immature and softer than those of adult dogs, and because their muscles are not yet fully developed. In addition, puppies are more susceptible to heat stress and cold injury than adult dogs because they have a greater surface area relative to their body weight. Even after the growth plates close, young dogs should not be worked strenuously until their muscles have been developed by a program of increasing exercise over a period of several months. Just as with human adolescents, canine adolescents need time to adapt to their new bodies and to develop coordination.

A conditioning program for a puppy should intermingle moderate exercise with brief training sessions and lots of play. It should also provide a great deal of variety and opportunities to experience different venues and to meet new people and other dogs. For example, when a puppy is very young, between seven and twelve weeks of age, you can play lots of fun exercise games such as "Climb Over and Crawl Under the Owner's Lap," "Chase That Rat-on-a-String," and "Steal the Toy from Big Brother." You could also walk around the block, go for a hike in the woods, play in a shallow creek, and begin to teach your puppy the foundations of jump training with poles on the ground. As he grows older, he will be able to walk for greater distances and play for longer periods of time without needing a rest. Throughout his adolescence, your puppy will have lots of energy and will want to be busy all of the time. His body will reach adult size, and you may be fooled into thinking that he has adult stamina. The trick at this stage is to give him abundant exercise, play lots of games, and give him many intellectual challenges — without overdoing it.

REGAINING CONDITION AFTER INJURY

Physiotherapy

Performance dogs, because they are athletes, are susceptible to a variety of types of injury. Injury to bones, if severe, can result in secondary injury to muscles and nerves. The muscles themselves are very responsive to use. When they are used, muscles increase in size. Disuse, either due to lack of exercise or injury to the muscles or to their nerve supply, causes muscles to shrink (atrophy). The first muscle fibers to shrink are the slow-twitch fibers, which are responsible for endurance. With prolonged disuse, the fast-twitch fibers, which provide strength, will also atrophy.

Muscle shrinking as a result of disuse or nerve injury can be slowed through physical therapy or massage. This type of treatment requires commitment on the part of the owner, but can be very rewarding. It can help a dog to become functional weeks or months before it would otherwise.

Heat and Massage

The goal of massage is to increase the circulation in the affected area and to stimulate the muscles, nerves, and other tissues. Massage is especially effective when preceded by heat treatment. Use moist, gentle heat (medium heat setting when using a heating pad). You should be able to put your hand under the source of the heat for five seconds without feeling discomfort. Animals with nerve damage may have impaired heat sensation, and even if they sense excessive heat, the nerve damage and muscle atrophy may prevent them from moving their limbs away to avoid being burned. There are many instances of severe burns resulting from dogs being left on heating pads.

If you are massaging a leg, support it with one hand or by resting the leg on a pillow so that the dog's muscles can relax and receive the proper benefit from the massage. If you are performing massage to treat arthritis or as therapy after joint surgery, you should massage all muscles above and below the joint. Start the massage by pressing down on the muscles with the heel of your palm. You should not move your hand over the skin, but instead press down hard enough to move the skin over the tissues below. Using the heel of your palm, it's unlikely that you will press too hard and possibly injure healing tissues. If the dog shows no discomfort with the palm massage, go back and massage the same areas with the balls of your fingers — not the tips, the balls (where your fingerprints are). This provides a deeper massage. Then run the flats of your hands over the whole massaged area. Finally, flex and extend the affected limb several times, gently, until a little resistance is felt. Support the joint while doing this to prevent any twisting of the limb.

Acupuncture Therapy

Older animals and animals that have had long athletic careers often have aches and pains, just as older people do. Traditional veterinary medicine often fails in its attempts to relieve chronic pain because of the frequent inability to identify the exact cause of the pain. In addition, painkillers act only temporarily, and most have significant side effects. Acupuncture has a definite place in the treatment of chronic pain, especially musculoskeletal pain, in dogs. Acupuncture provides pain relief in many cases where conventional therapy has failed.

The basic principle of acupuncture rests on the theory that there are specific points in the body that, if stimulated, will produce one or more physi-ological effects. When several points are stimulated correctly, the effects may be more than additive. The dog has at least 150 acupuncture points. The exact biochemical and molecular effects of acupuncture are not yet known, but it is thought that acupuncture stimulates the nerves that send messages to pain receptors in the brain. There are different kinds of nerve fibers. Some transmit pain sensation, while others do not. It is believed that the messages from acu-puncture stimulation are sent up nerves that do not transmit pain impulses, and these messages fill up the pain receptors so that they can no longer receive pain messages. Another theory suggests that acupuncture stimulation causes the localized secretion of chemicals which have both local and systemic effects that reduce pain. There is good evidence for both of these theories, and it may well be that they act together.

The practice of veterinary acupuncture is rapidly growing in North America. The most common uses for acupuncture therapy are: 1) relief of pain secondary to spinal cord degenerative disease or trauma, 2) relief of pain due to hip dysplasia, arthritis, and other degenerative joint diseases, and 3) treatment of chronic conditions, such as allergies, peripheral nerve damage, and others which have not responded to traditional treatment. Just as in more conventional forms of veterinary medicine, it should be remembered that acupuncture is a treatment and does not replace an adequate diagnosis.

In acupuncture, needles are used to penetrate the tissue at the acupunc-ture points. The tissue may be stimulated by twirling the needles or by applying an electrical stimulus. Water, electrolyte solutions, and other substances may be injected into the site through needles. Ultrasound may also be used to stimulate the points. There are several related techniques that are included in the broad classification of acupuncture. One is acupressure, in which finger pressure is applied to pressure points on the body. Acupuncture treatments generally need to be repeated, usually once or twice a week, for several weeks. Some improve-ment should be noted within a few days after the treatment and certainly by the third or fourth treatment.

Some of the possible side effects of acupuncture treatment include the chance of injuring a vital organ, bleeding, and infection. Some people complain that their dogs are initially worse for the first few days after acupuncture treatment. This is usually because the dog was overtreated. Either too many points were used, the wrong needles were used, or they were left in place too long. If you decide to pursue this form of treatment, take your dog to an experienced veterinary acupuncturist. To date, the American Veterinary Medical Association has no formal certification program for veterinary acupuncturists. However, the International Association of Veterinary Acupuncturists provides education and accreditation for veterinarians. Personal recommendations are invaluable in helping to locate a skilled acupuncturist.

Chiropractic Therapy

Canine chiropractic treatment is based on the theory that misalignment of bones can cause strain on the muscles and joints and on the nerves that serve them. This results in muscle tension and further misalignment of bones and sets up a vicious cycle of musculoskeletal pain from musculoskeletal compensation. Chiropractic adjustment may be especially helpful in dogs that are predominantly one-sided — always tending to turn to either the right or the left. This can occur in dogs that are always worked on the handler's left as in obedience or in dogs that sidewind (crab) when trotting. This results in an uneven tension of muscles and misalignment of the skeletal system. Chiropractic adjustment realigns the bones, helping to relax the muscles and return balance to the musculoskeletal system. There should be some visible effects of chiropractic adjustment after the first or second treatment. It is essential to rely on personal recommendations from others when choosing a canine chiropractor.

Other Nontraditional Therapeutic Modalities

There are a number of other therapeutic modalities that have been used in horses and humans and are beginning to be used in dogs. These include electromagnetic therapy, ultrasound, transcutaneous electrical nerve stimulation, magnetic field therapy, and laser therapy. Many of these are still in the experimental stages, and their effectiveness has not been studied using properly controlled clinical trials. Nevertheless, these nontraditional therapies can be useful as a supplement but not a replacement for traditional treatments.

Additional Reading

L. L. Blythe, J. R. Gannon, A. M. Craig. *Care of the Racing Greyhound. A Guide for Trainers, Breeders and Veterinarians*. American Greyhound Council, Inc. 1994.

Mary Jo Sminkey

A Soft-Coated Wheaten Terrier sailing through an agility course. For owners and trainers of performance dogs, an understanding of lameness and injury is imperative.

6.

LAMENESS AND

PERFORMANCE-RELATED INJURIES

All in the town were still asleep
When the sun came up with a shout and a leap.
In the lonely streets, unseen by man,
A little dog danced
And the day began.

Rupert Brooke

STRUCTURE OF THE BONES AND JOINTS

There are two kinds of bones: long bones, like the bones of the legs, and flat bones, like the bones of the skull. The flat bones grow larger in many directions at once, whereas the long bones have a specific area at one or both ends called the growth plate, where the cells replicate and add to the length of the bone. This growth plate is an area in which the bone is softer and more readily injured. The growth plate continues to add to the length of the bone until the age at which it is genetically programmed to close. It then becomes identical in composition to the rest of the bone. The age at which the growth plates close differs for each bone (Table 6.1). Larger dogs' growth plates close later than those of small dogs.

The long bones are usually narrower in the middle and wider at the ends. Engineering studies have demonstrated that this shape efficiently absorbs the stresses of weight, especially when combined with movement. Look at the supports for bridges and you will see this same pattern of a wider support that narrows as it meets the horizontal road above. The long bones have a dense outer cortex, and inside they have a cavity with smaller, crisscrossing pieces of

Table 6.1 Times at Which the Growth Plates Close	
Bone	*Age at Fusion*
Humerus at shoulder joint	10 to 12 months
Radius at the elbow joint	9 to 11 months
Bones of the toes	6 to 7 months
Pelvic bones	5 to 6 months
Femur at the hip joint	9 to 11 months
Tibia at the stifle joint	10 to 14 months

bone. Many people think of bone as a stable tissue because it is so hard. But, in fact, the bone is always changing in response to the stresses placed upon it. If a dog places more weight on the inside of its leg, the bone will begin to thicken in that area, eventually remodeling itself to cope with the increased weight.

The joints are complex structures, designed to permit the bones to move against each other with as little friction as possible while keeping them in close approximation. This friction-free movement is achieved by the cartilage covering the ends of the bone and the synovial fluid that bathes it. The synovial fluid has properties similar to the oil in an engine, which lets the pistons pump up and down in the cylinders billions of times without wearing out. The synovial fluid is retained in the joint cavity by the joint capsule, a tough tissue sac surrounding the entire joint. Some joints, such as the knee joint, also have menisci, crescent-shaped pieces of cartilage that sit between the bones and help reduce the pressure of bone against bone. Bones are held together by ligaments, dense bands of tissue which have a great deal of tensile strength. These ligaments may be present within the joint capsule or outside of it. Different joints have different degrees of flexibility. For example, the carpal (wrist) joint is much more flexible than the tarsal (hock) joint. In addition, the amount of flexibility in a given joint differs from dog to dog. Flexibility is important so that the dog can perform the full range of motions with the joint. Too much flexibility, however, can make joints more susceptible to injury and degenerative joint disease.

HOW TO EVALUATE LAMENESS
Lameness can be caused by pain in the bones, muscles, tendons, ligaments, or nerves, or by a mechanical problem affecting function. There are many causes of lameness, and just a few are listed in Table 6.2.

Table 6.2
Common Causes of Lameness in Dogs

Classification	Example
Congenital Disorders	Conformational abnormalities
	Patellar luxation
Degenerative Disorders	Degenerative joint disease
	Intervertebral disk disease
	Spondylosis
	Cervical vertebral instability
	(Wobbler syndrome)
Genetic Disorders	Hip dysplasia
	Osteochondrosis
	Elbow dysplasia
Traumatic Disorders	Fracture
	Luxation
	Sprain
	Strain
	Intervertebral disk herniation
	Muscle lacerations
	Ruptured cruciate ligaments
	Traumatic peripheral neuropathy
Infectious Diseases	Lyme disease
Unknown Cause	Panosteitis

Sudden lameness should be evaluated at once. In some cases, such as with cut pads, the cause can be identified immediately. In other cases, veterinary evaluation may be necessary. A lame dog should not be permitted to train or compete until a diagnosis has been made, even though the dog may be willing. Lameness is usually indicative of pain. But a dog may be so keen to train or play that it will exercise despite considerable pain. Letting such a dog exercise, however, is risky, as it can lead to further injury and may prolong the time required for healing.

To evaluate lameness, first observe the dog while standing. Note whether the leg hangs in its correct position and whether the dog is willing to bear weight on the leg. Have the dog move a few feet forward and stand again. Stand in front of and behind the dog and check to see if he is leaning to one side or the other. Notice the pattern in which the dog places the legs. Does he always stand with one leg ahead of the other? If so, it may be because he doesn't want to bear weight on that leg. Sometimes, reduced weight-bearing is

very subtle and can be detected only by observing a difference in the shape of
the foot or by finding that one leg is more easily moved out of position than the
others. Normally, dogs bear about 65 percent of their weight on the front legs
and 35 percent on the rear legs. If a dog has pain in a rear leg, it may lean
forward and bear more weight on the front legs. If the pain is present for a long
period of time, such as in dogs with hip dysplasia, the dog can eventually bear
up to 90% of its weight on the front legs. A dog with long-standing hip dysplasia may have very overdeveloped front leg musculature and atrophied (reduced
in size) muscles of the rear legs.

The lame dog should then be moved at a walk and, if it is not too painful,
at a trot. Sometimes it may be necessary to have the dog walk or trot in a tight
circle, pivoting to one side and then to the other, before the lameness becomes
obvious. Going up or down stairs may also make a subtle lameness more obvious. The dog should be observed from the front, side, and rear. The dog will try
to bear less weight on the painful leg and will shift more weight to the opposite
limb. For a front leg lameness, the dog will lift his head when the painful leg is
on the ground (to reduce the amount of weight borne on that leg) and will lower
its head when the good limb is bearing weight (Figure 6.1). For a rear leg
lameness, it is helpful to crouch down and view the pelvis from behind as the
dog trots away. Like the head, the pelvis will be raised when the dog bears
weight on the painful limb. In addition, the length of stride of the sound limb
may be normal or increased while that of the painful limb may be shortened to
reduce the time during which the painful limb bears weight. Injuries to the
shoulder and hip have the greatest effect on the dog's stride length. In addition,
the dog may drag its toenails, stumble, or cross the legs over each other when
gaiting. One very helpful test in determining lameness is to place the dog's two
front or two rear feet on a paper sprinkled with corn starch, then have the dog
trot away on a surface such as black or green matting where the imprints of the
feet will show up. The foot of the lame leg will leave a smaller print, and you
may be able to measure the difference in stride length using a yardstick.

Once the affected limb has been identified, the limb should be carefully
palpated. Look for any swellings or abnormal shape and try to locate, if possible, the source of the pain. Run your hands down both legs simultaneously to
feel for swellings or areas of increased heat on the affected leg, particularly
checking in the areas of the joints. An enlarged area usually indicates inflammation. An area on one leg that is smaller than the other may mean there has been a
loss of muscle mass, usually due to disuse. Each joint should be flexed and
extended in turn to look for a reduction or an increase in range of motion which
may result from a fracture, luxation, sprain, or degenerative joint disease. The

Fig. 6.1. Lameness in a dog. As the affected forefoot bears weight (A), the head lifts up and back in order to shift weight backward and off the affected limb. The diagonal rear leg also moves a bit more forward to get under the shifted center of gravity and to reduce the weight borne by the affected leg. The opposite (unaffected) foreleg stays on the ground a trifle longer to reduce the amount of time that the affected leg bears weight. As the sound limb accepts the weight (B), the head moves forward and down to shift weight off the affected limb as quickly as possible. The stride length is shortened in order to lengthen the amount of time that the sound limb is on the ground and to lessen the impact on the affected limb.

pads and the skin between the toes should be carefully examined for cuts or the presence of foreign bodies such as thorns or burrs. The dog should then be laid on its side and the leg examined again. This second examination with the dog in a more relaxed position can reveal abnormalities that were obscured by muscular tension, but it can be harder to compare one leg to the other in this position.

Lameness evaluation can help you detect foreign bodies (particularly common in the foot), sprains, and severe muscle injury (detected as swelling over the affected area), fractures (detected as crunching noises and evidence of severe pain when the affected leg is moved), and joint disease (reduced range of motion of the affected joint, often accompanied by pain).

Any performance dog with a persistent or recurring lameness should be evaluated as soon as possible by a qualified veterinarian. The veterinarian should perform a complete examination, including a lameness evaluation as described above, and may wish to do tests on the blood and/or urine as well. The evaluation may also include radiographs (X-rays) and perhaps a neurological examination. If your veterinarian is unable to make a definitive diagnosis of the cause of the lameness, you may wish to be referred to a veterinary orthopedic specialist, especially if the lameness is severe or has persisted for over a week. Peak function of the limbs is a prerequisite for a performance career, and it is always prudent to diagnose any problem as early as possible.

COMMON CAUSES OF LAMENESS - JOINTS

Degenerative Joint Disease

Degenerative joint disease, or osteoarthritis, is very common in older performance dogs. Throughout a performance career, the bones of the joints are constantly rubbing against each other and, over time, this causes wear. This normal wear and tear can be exacerbated by trauma, genetic predisposition, obesity, exercise, and other factors. The tissues of the joints try to repair the damage with varying success; sometimes the repair efforts also cause problems. Estimates are that approximately 20 percent of older dogs have degenerative joint disease of the stifle (knee), shoulder, and/or elbow joints. Degenerative joint disease has shortened or ended many a performance dog's career.

There are two classifications of degenerative joint disease: primary and secondary. Primary degenerative joint disease occurs in joints that have normal structure but which have had excessive use, such as the joints of an older dog or an obese dog (Figs. 6.2, 6.3). Secondary degenerative joint disease occurs when there is an abnormality of the bones or joint that predisposes the dog to development of osteoarthritis. Abnormalities in bone conformation such as straight stifles, hyperextension of the hock, and bone deformities can put great stress on the joints. For example, a dog that is pigeon-toed applies a twisting motion to the joints of the carpus and feet with each step. In addition, most of the weight is borne on the outside of the foot. This strain, over the life of the animal, will predispose it to degenerative joint disease of the carpus and the joints of the feet. In some breeds, conformational abnormalities have been built into the dog, such that their joints continuously undergo additional stress. For example, the chondrodysplastic breeds (dwarfs) such as the Pekingese, the Basset Hound, and the Dachshund usually do not have straight bones in the front limbs. The radius and ulna are shortened and rotated, and this puts additional stress on the elbow and on the carpus. Because of their structure, these breeds are more likely to develop degeneration of some joints.

Secondary degenerative joint disease can also develop as a result of joint abnormalities that increase the wear and tear on joints. Some conditions of the joint that predispose a dog to degenerative joint disease include hip dysplasia, elbow dysplasia, osteochondrosis dissecans, ruptured cruciate ligaments, and patellar luxation. These are discussed individually later in this chapter.

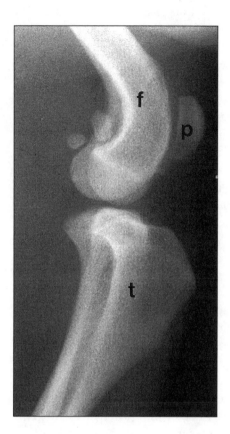

Fig. 6.2. Normal stifle joint: f—femur, t—tibia, p—patella. The two small bones behind the joint are the fabellae.

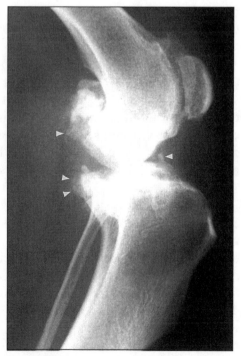

Fig. 6.3. Degenerative joint disease of the stifle of an overweight Labrador Retriever. Instead of the smooth joint surfaces of the normal stifle joint, bony growths have formed over the joint surface and at the edge of the joint (arrowheads). These cause pain and impair joint function.

One of the first signs of degenerative joint disease in a performance dog may be a change in the dog's performance. For example, one day the dog might refuse to jump. Perhaps, if encouraged, it will then jump, and it may show no unwillingness for the rest of the session. These sometimes subtle signs may be the first clue that a dog is suffering from degenerative joint disease. The dog may also be stiff or lame, particularly after a period of sustained activity or after resting following activity. Generally, after the dog has returned to moderate activity, the lameness disappears. A dog with severe degenerative joint disease may be constantly lame and may become irritable, especially towards children, and may bite when touched. Sometimes dogs in severe pain will actually have a different facial expression. This occurred in a friend's dog which was euthanized at two years of age for severe hip dysplasia. When awake, the dog had an intense expression which made his face wrinkled and unpleasant-looking. The owner thought that this was just the dog's natural expression until after the dog was put to sleep. Then his face relaxed, and the dog regained the typical kindly expression for which his breed is known.

Degenerative joint disease is best diagnosed by a veterinarian who should perform a complete physical examination and should carefully check each joint for range of motion and for signs of pain. The veterinarian will also perform a radiographic evaluation on the dog and may take blood and/or urine for further testing. Note that a lack of changes on a radiograph does not mean that the dog doesn't have arthritis or that it doesn't suffer joint pain. The main objective of this diagnostic procedure is to try to determine whether the degenerative joint disease is primary (from just plain wear and tear) or secondary (related to genetic, infectious, traumatic, or other problems). If the disease is secondary, treatment should be aimed at controlling the cause of the degenerative joint disease, if possible. For example, if the dog has a ruptured anterior cruciate ligament, unless the ligament is repaired surgically, the dog stands little chance of regaining full function of the knee joint. Without treatment, its performance career will be significantly hampered.

Once a diagnosis of degenerative joint disease has been made and surgical treatment has been undertaken if possible, continuing medical treatment centers around the following: adequate periods of rest, avoidance of overexertion of affected joints, maintenance of a normal body weight, moderate exercise, and pain relief if necessary. For performance dogs, the decision as to what constitutes adequate rest, avoidance of overexertion, and moderate exercise can be difficult. Such dogs are accustomed to a great deal of physical activity and often will overexert themselves in spite of severe pain in order to please their owners or because of sheer enjoyment of the activity. Owners must be constantly aware of and sensitive to this. There is no cure for degenerative joint disease, and treatment consists of reducing the amount of continuing damage to the joints and giving the joints more time to repair. Balancing rest with controlled exercise is essential to maintain muscle tone and to keep the joints from stiffening up. One of the best controlled exercises is walking on a leash. Depending on the severity of the arthritis, the dog can be jogged or allowed to walk at its own pace. For dogs with severe arthritis, walks can be interspersed with rest, and the daily exercise should include periods of controlled play. The best play that a dog with degenerative joint disease can undertake is swimming. Swimming exercises the muscles without stressing the joints by weight-bearing. Heat and gentle massage (see Chapter 5) are beneficial in relieving muscle spasm and pain.

Analgesics (painkillers) should be administered only when necessary, and treated dogs should be exercised carefully to avoid further damage to the joints. Aspirin is the most commonly used analgesic, and it can be quite effective. It can, however, cause stomach upset and even ulcers. Enteric-coated or buffered aspirin can help to prevent this. Administering the analgesic on a full stomach may also help to prevent stomach upset. Great care should be taken when treating a dog with analgesics for a long period of time. Painkillers may clear up the lameness, since the dog will use the limb if it feels no pain. However, they may also mask an ongoing problem that can then become worse because the dog uses the injured limb.

Carprophen (Rimadyl®) is a new anti-inflammatory product for alleviation of arthritis pain in dogs. It is reported to be highly effective and to have minimal side effects in the majority of dogs. At this writing, however, there have been some reports of liver damage in treated dogs, so be sure to consult with your veterinarian before treating your dog.

Butazolidine is another analgesic that has been used for many years in the treatment of severe, chronic joint pain in dogs. Because it can cause kidney failure in dogs, it should be used only intermittently or as a last resort.

Numerous oral nutriceutical products have arrived on the market in the mid-1990's. Nutriceuticals are substances that occur naturally, as opposed to pharmaceuticals, which are drugs designed by pharmaceutical firms. A number of these are highly effective in reducing arthritis pain and even in aiding repair of damaged joints. These products are derived from naturally occurring substances such as the green-lipped mussel (*Perna cannaliculus*), ground shark or bovine cartilage, and other source. Their active ingredients include polysulfated glycosaminoglycans, glucosamine, and chondroitin sulfate. These molecules form the building blocks of cartilage and joint fluid. A related product (Adequan®) has been available for many years in an injectable form, and its effectiveness has been demonstrated in controlled, scientific trials. However, the oral forms of these drugs are a more recent addition to the market. Since these products are derived from naturally occurring substances, they cannot be patented, although specific mixtures of nutriceuticals can be. These products are not produced or sold by the major pharmaceutical firms, which design new biochemicals. At this writing, there are many mixes of nutriceuticals on the market. Many also include antioxidants, which may help to reduce the amount of ongoing damage to joints from free radicals. However, those that have added vitamins and minerals, particularly large amounts of calcium, should be avoided.

Nutriceuticals can dramatically reduce the pain of arthritis, although sometimes it may take 6 to 8 weeks for full effect. Some people have reported that their dogs showed no or minimal improvement with treatment but appeared to have more pain when treatment was stopped. Perhaps those dogs were stoically accepting the pain before treatment but noticed the pain more after cessation of treatment. In any case, antiarthritic nutriceuticals can be helpful to dogs with known arthritis or with conditions that result in arthritis, such as hip or elbow dysplasia. I treat all of my dogs after the age of 8 years on the assumption that older dogs have aches and pains due to arthritis just as older, active humans do. I do not treat my puppies or adult dogs without cause or as a preventive, because I am concerned that such treatment might obscure clinical signs when problems do occur, and prevent me from arriving at a timely diagnosis.

Steroids should not be administered for the treatment of lameness without first making a diagnosis. If your dog is lame and has had a veterinary examination, but the cause of the lameness has not been identified, do not allow steroids to be administered. Steroids may reduce inflammation which can cause pain, and they also give the dog a feeling of euphoria, which may make it feel like exercising more. But they can also cause immunosuppression, weakening the dog's defense mechanisms. If the dog is lame because of an infection in the bone or joint, this immunosuppression may allow the infectious agent to replicate unchecked, causing much more severe disease. In addition, longterm steroid administration should be avoided in most dogs with degenerative joint disease because steroids interfere with repair processes.

Several years ago, a friend had a Doberman Pinscher, Mocha, who was competing in obedience trials for her Companion Dog Excellent title. One day Mocha refused to jump over the high jump. My friend then noticed that the dog was lame in one rear leg. When Mocha was rested, the lameness went away, but it returned occasionally over the next several days. My friend took the dog's temperature and noted that she had an intermittent, mild fever. She then took the dog to a local veterinarian and gave him the dog's clinical history. The veterinarian examined the dog briefly but could find no abnormalities. He also disregarded the importance of the intermittent fever. Without doing further tests or evaluation of the lameness, he injected Mocha with steroids and sent her home. Mocha died several days later in the intensive care unit of a veterinary school with a fungal infection which, because of the immunosuppression caused by the steroids, had spread from a joint throughout her body, to her lungs, brain, and liver. This tragic story is presented here, not only as an example of poor veterinary care, but as a warning about the serious consequences of casual use of corticosteroids.

Osteochondrosis (OCD)

This is an important cause of lameness in dogs. Although it can occur in just about any joint, it is most common in the shoulder joint. Affected dogs may be lame in only one leg, but it is thought that a large percentage of dogs with osteochondrosis have lesions in other joints as well. Osteochondrosis is most common in large, fast-growing dogs and first becomes evident around six to nine months of age, although it can occur in dogs as old as two or three years. The lameness is often first noted after severe exercise, but it may also come on gradually. It is characterized by a shortening of the swing phase of the gait and is most noticeable at a walk.

The exact cause of osteochondrosis is not known, but it is thought that both heredity and nutrition contribute to its development. Studies of osteochondrosis in both horses and dogs have shown that it can be induced by feeding diets with very high levels of energy, protein, and minerals.

In osteochondrosis, alterations in the blood supply cause the cartilage of the affected joint to become weak, develop fissures, and separate from the underlying bone, leaving a defect. This increases the friction of the bones rubbing against each other. Increased or abnormal use of the joint may cause the damaged cartilage to chip away from the underlying bone. The piece of cartilage then floats around inside the joint cavity. Sometimes it reattaches, or it may be reabsorbed by the body. Frequently the piece of cartilage remains in the joint as a painful foreign body. The damage to the cartilage and to the underlying bone, if not repaired, will lead to degenerative joint disease.

A diagnosis of OCD involves performing careful radiography to demonstrate the defect in the surface of the joint (Figs. 6.4, 6.5). But sometimes

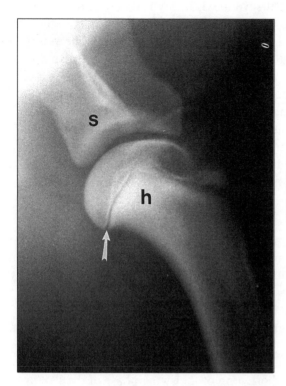

Fig. 6.4. Normal shoulder joint: s—scapula, h—humerus. Arrow indicates the space where the growth plate has not yet closed in this young animal.

Fig. 6.5. Osteochondrosis in the shoulder joint of a Great Dane. There is a defect in the cartilage of the humerus which can be seen as a darker area (outlined by arrow-heads).

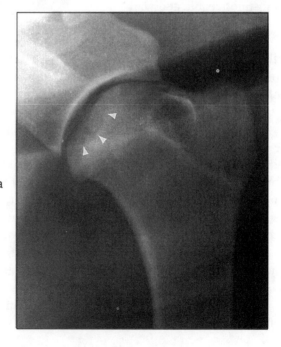

radiographs do not reveal the defect. Veterinarians may suggest conservative treatment in which the dog is rested for weeks or months until the cartilage has healed and any detached pieces of cartilage have been reabsorbed. For a performance dog, however, surgical intervention permits a more rapid return to function and reduces the chances of early development of degenerative joint disease. If there is a large piece of damaged cartilage in the joint, it should definitely be removed surgically. During surgery, the surgeon will clean off the cartilaginous surfaces of the bones to smooth them out and thus reduce the chances of degenerative joint disease.

Hip Dysplasia

This problem has been identified in most breeds of dogs but is more common in breeds weighing over 40 pounds. Both sexes are affected equally. The inheritance of hip dysplasia is complex, probably involving many genes. Some believe that the genes do not affect the skeleton directly but affect the ligaments and supporting structures of the hip, causing laxity (looseness) of the hip joint. Dysplastic dogs are born with normal hips (Fig. 6.6), but the hips become loose at some point during growth. The joint laxity causes abnormal stresses on the joint, and both the acetabulum (hip socket) and the head of the femur undergo changes in response to those stresses. The acetabulum eventually becomes flatter, while the head of the femur becomes less rounded and develops a thickened neck. As the condition progresses, degenerative joint disease develops, and bony growths (exostoses) appear on the head of the femur and around the rim of the acetabulum.

Hip dysplasia can include any or all of the following changes in the hip joint: joint laxity (Fig. 6.7), subluxation of the femoral head, in which the femoral head is not held tightly against the acetabulum (Fig. 6.8), rupture of the ligament that holds the femur into the hip joint (Fig. 6.9), shallow acetabulum (Fig. 6.10), thickening of the neck of the femur (Fig. 6.11), flattening of the femoral head, and degenerative joint disease (Fig. 6.12).

Both genetics and environment contribute to the development of hip dysplasia. Puppies that grow rapidly, and especially those that are overweight, are more likely to develop hip dysplasia. The genes for hip dysplasia have not been identified yet, and it is certain to be a difficult task because the condition is so widespread in the canine population, and there are likely many genes that modify expression of disease. Thus, a dog can carry the genes for hip dysplasia but have normal hips. There are also many environmental factors that have been shown to increase the development or expression of canine hip dysplasia. These include rapid growth, high caloric intake during growth, and supplementation with minerals. The severity and incidence of hip dysplasia can be reduced by restricting the growth rate of puppies. Slowing the rate of growth allows better formation of bone, and keeping the weight down lessens the stress on the joints.

There are three main registries in North America that certify dogs as free of radiographic signs of hip dysplasia by their criteria. Table 6.3 provides a comparison of the three registries and their requirements. The Orthopedic Foundation for Animals (OFA) is the oldest registry. It has examined thousands of radiographs and has established a grading system for hip conformation. Using their criteria, normal hips should have a cup-shaped acetabulum into which the rounded femoral head fits closely. At least 50 percent of the femoral head should be within the acetabulum in the radiograph. Hips graded as "excellent" have nearly perfect conformation, with the head of the femur tight in the socket. Those graded as "good" have normal conformation for that particular age and breed of dog (see Fig. 6.6). Dogs with "fair" hips are within normal limits but are less than ideal. In a dog classified as "borderline," there are possible abnormalities, and the evaluator would like to see if there is any change over the next 6 months. Dysplastic hips may be classified as mild, moderate, or severe. However, these degrees of severity may reflect environmental influences more than heredity. That is, the dog is dysplastic, but because of obesity, excessive exercise, or other reasons has greater bony changes than another dog. If the hips cannot be adequately assessed because of poor positioning of the dog during the radiographic procedure, or because of poor exposure or development of the film (this is true of fully 10 percent of the radiographs submitted to the OFA), they will be referred to as "indeterminate," and the owner will be advised to have the hips radiographed again.

Although your veterinarian may provide an opinion of your dog's hip conformation, you should always obtain the OFA's evaluation. This is essential because breeds differ in their normal hip conformation, and the radiologists for the OFA read many more radiographs from dogs of your breed than veterinarians in general practice.

The OFA performed a retrospective study to determine how well preliminary radiographic evaluation predicted the dog's hip status at two years. They compared hip gradings of thousands of dogs that had preliminary radiographs taken between five and 23 months of age to the gradings of the same dogs after 24 months. Ninety percent of dogs that were clear of hip dysplasia at five to 23 month were also clear after the age of two. Of the remaining 10 percent, four percent had better hips at the age of two years, and six percent were graded dysplastic. Thus, although the OFA will not provide certification that the dog is

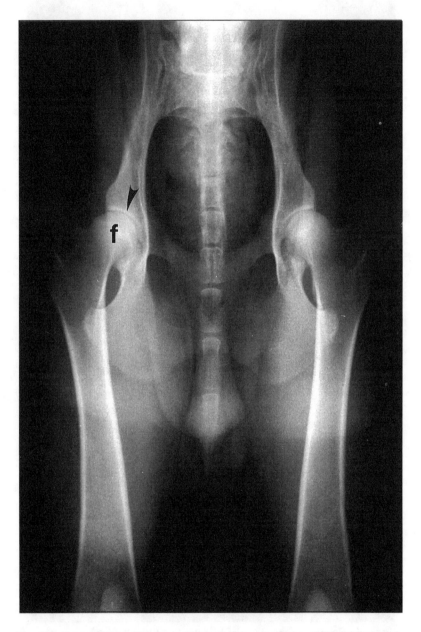

Fig. 6.6. Normal hips. The femoral head (f) is rounded and fits tightly into the acetabulum (hip socket—arrowhead). More than 50 percent of the femoral head is within the socket.

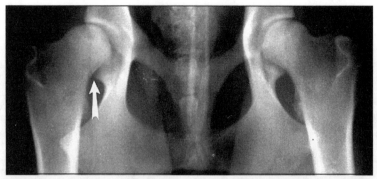

Fig. 6.7. Hip dysplasia. There is joint laxity of the hip on the left. Less than 50 percent of the femoral head is within the socket.

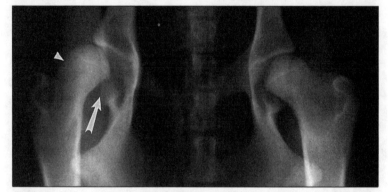

Fig. 6.8. Severe hip dysplasia. There is subluxation of the femoral head. The femur on the left is almost completely out of the socket. In addition, the left acetabulum is flattened (arrow) and the neck of the femur is thickened (arrowhead).

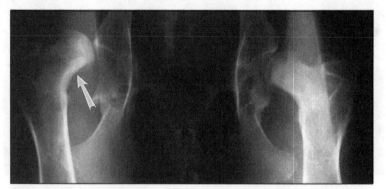

Fig. 6.9. Severe hip dysplasia. The femur on the left is so badly luxated (arrow) that the teres ligament that holds the femur in the socket is probably ruptured (although ligaments cannot be seen on an X-ray). Flattened acetabula, thickening of the neck of the femur and bony changes can also be seen.

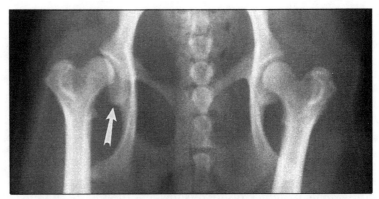

Fig. 6.10. Hip dysplasia. The acetabulum on the left is flattened.

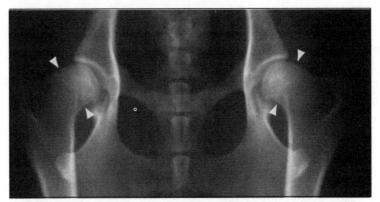

Fig. 6.11. Hip dysplasia. The necks of both femurs are thickened (arrowheads).

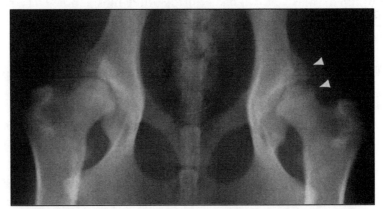

Fig. 6.12. Hip dysplasia demonstrating the bony changes characteristic of degenerative joint disease (arrowheads). Note: All of the above radiographs are from different breeds, from a Rottweiler to a Pekingese.

Table 6.3 Comparison of Hip Registries				
Organization	Age at Prelim. X-ray	Clearance Age	Hip Position	Scale
OFA	5 to 23 months	24 months	Extended	Normal: Excellent, Good, Fair Dysplastic: Mild, Moderate, Severe
OVC	Not applicable	18 months	Extended	Clear/Dysplastic
PennHip	4 months	Not applicable	Flexed	Percentile - compared to others of the same breed

clear of radiographic evidence of hip dysplasia until after 24 months, a preliminary OFA evaluation has significant predictive value.

If your dog has evidence of hip laxity or arthritis at a young age, it is
important to consider your surgical and medical options before the condition has
progressed further. In particular, one of the best surgical options for severely
dysplastic dogs, triple pelvic osteotomy, must be performed before the development of arthritic changes in the hip joints. Most dysplastic dogs have arthritic
changes by the age of two years. Further, your dog will likely be training and
perhaps even competing before the age of two years. If you know he has hip
dysplasia, you can take extra care to moderate his exercise and target his conditioning program to strengthen his rear legs and spinal muscles to compensate for
the hip joints which are not functioning at peak efficiency.

The OFA tracked working dogs in the Armed Forces that were certified
free of hip dysplasia at two years of age. Fewer than one percent of dogs certified free of hip dysplasia at two had arthritis of the hips at nine. The results of
this study suggest that OFA certification is valuable in predicting whether your
dog will develop arthritis.

The Ontario Veterinary College (OVC) in Canada also has a hip certification program. Like the OFA, the dog's hips are radiographed with the legs
extended. However, the OVC will provide certification on dogs as early as 18
months of age. In addition, they do not classify the dog's hip conformation as
excellent, good, or fair. Instead, they classify the hips as dysplastic or not.

The PennHip technique provides a very different perspective on hip
dysplasia. This technique measures laxity in the hip joint, thought to be the
initial alteration that eventually leads to arthritis. Instead of stating whether
your dog is dysplastic or not, the PennHip report compares the degree of laxity
(looseness) in your dog's hips to that of others of his breed. The principle is that

if you breed your dog only if it has a better score than most others in the breed and only to an individual with a better score, you will reduce the incidence of hip dysplasia in your lines. The advantages of the PennHip system are that dogs can be tested at a younger age (although not much younger than for preliminary OFA evaluation), and they need be tested only once. On the other hand, at least at the time of writing, PennHip evaluations cannot be used as a basis for deciding whether to perform surgical procedures such as triple pelvis osteotomy. In addition, far fewer dogs have been tested using this method are than by the OFA. This makes it difficult to determine the significance of their findings, particularly in the rarer breeds. Further, there are no baseline data for mixed breeds. At this writing there is only a limited number of veterinarians in the United States who are certified to perform the procedure. Therefore, at least at present, PennHip evaluations are of more value for breeders than for those interested in evaluating their performance dogs.

The clinical signs of hip dysplasia often first occur when the dog is between six and 18 months of age. The dog may yelp in pain during strenuous exercise or may become periodically lame in the rear. Frequently, the pain will disappear for years, showing up again only when the dog is older, at which time the dog may again become lame and stiff as a result of degenerative joint disease. Dogs with hip dysplasia may stand with their rear legs close together and with the stifles bent inward, and they may walk stiffly. Other signs of hip dysplasia may include a bunny-hopping gait, trouble negotiating stairs or slick floors, and difficulty standing up after resting.

There is little, if any, correlation between the clinical signs of hip dysplasia and the severity of the changes in the hip. Many dogs with hip dysplasia show no signs of pain. In one survey of 68 dogs in which hip dysplasia was diagnosed at an early age, 76 percent had only minimal gait abnormalities a little over four years later. The other 24 percent developed lameness and gait abnormalities at a young age.

There is no cure for hip dysplasia. However, there are several surgical options that should be considered. The first, and perhaps most successful in returning a severely dysplastic performance dog to an active career, is triple pelvic osteotomy (TPO). This involves cutting the pelvic bone and reshaping it so that the acetabulum forms a better seat for the ball of the femur. This surgical procedure is best performed on dogs that have evidence of significant laxity but no bony changes indicating arthritis. The majority of dogs that undergo TPO are able to return to training and have a full performance career.

Another surgical option for returning a dog to a working career is total hip replacement. This involves removing the dysplastic hip and fitting the dog with a prosthesis. The major disadvantages of total hip replacement are that it is much more expensive than TPO and cannot be performed in dogs less than 40 pounds. This is the surgery of choice for dogs that already have arthritic changes in the hip joints.

The third surgical option is femoral head osteotomy. In this procedure, the femoral heads are removed and, with time, a false joint forms from scar tissue around the remaining bone. This surgery is essentially a salvage procedure used to relieve the dog of the pain of bone rubbing against bone. Dogs that have had this procedure performed on both hips should not be returned to a performance career because the false joints that form are not stable enough. However, it is remarkable how well this procedure can alleviate pain in dogs with severe hip dysplasia.

Treatment of dogs with mild to moderate pain due to hip dysplasia generally consists of rest, moderate exercise of a type that puts minimal stress on the hips (swimming is ideal), and analgesics as necessary to relieve pain. Dogs with hip dysplasia should not be allowed to become overweight, as this increases the stress on the joints. At one time it was thought that dogs with hip dysplasia should be exercised heavily to develop a strong muscle mass to support the weakened hip joint. However, it is now thought that moderate, preferably non-weight-bearing exercise is better. Studies of young children (with normal hips) have shown that excessive athletic activity may contribute to the development of degenerative joint disease of the hip, which appears later in life. It would seem, therefore, that dogs with abnormal hips should be exercised gently.

The chronic pain and instability of arthritis causes the dogs to stress the muscles of the spine and legs, and this can result in misalignment of the bones. Thus, chiropractic adjustments should be considered in dogs with hip dysplasia. Acupuncture is also frequently helpful in reducing the pain of hip dysplasia.

Ultimately, the best treatment for dogs with hip dysplasia lies in prevention, and this involves the breeding of only dogs with radiographically normal hips. It should be noted, however, that phenotype (radiographic appearance of hips) is not necessarily an accurate reflection of genotype (the genes for hip conformation). Hence, a dog with radiographically normal hips can still carry genes for hip dysplasia. This is why two OFA "good" dogs can be bred and still produce dysplastic offspring. However, selection based on hip evaluation can significantly reduce the incidence of hip dysplasia as evidenced by the fact that only 8 to 10 percent of the dogs produced by Guide Dogs for the Blind (which for many years has bred only dogs with normal hips) are dysplastic. These statistics are much lower than the national averages for any of the three breeds which Guide Dogs for the Blind produce (Labrador Retrievers, Golden Retrievers, and German Shepherd Dogs). In addition, a number of breeds have improved the overall quality of hips over the last several years by a rigorous program of breeding only radiographically normal dogs.

Elbow Dysplasia

This term is used to describe a constellation of abnormalities of the elbow joint that may occur alone or in combination. The three abnormalities are ununited anconeal process, osteochondrosis of the elbow, and fragmentation of the medial coronoid process (Figs. 6.13, 6.14), all bony changes that contribute to instability and increased friction in the elbow. These abnormalities ultimately result in degenerative joint disease of the elbow. There is probably a genetic predisposition to these problems, and the condition occurs with greater frequency in large, rapidly growing dogs. All three problems are thought to be related to abnormalities in the conformation of the elbow joint that develop as the dog grows. Generally, the first signs of lameness occur at about six to nine months of age. An affected dog may be clearly lame on one front leg, it may have only mild signs such as a reluctance to play, or it may have no clinical signs at all. There is no cure *per se*, but some relief can be obtained through surgical intervention in certain of the abnormalities. Because the front legs bear twice as much weight as the rear legs, dogs with elbow dysplasia often have more severe lameness than those with rear leg problems. It is unlikely that a dog with elbow dysplasia will perform well into old age because of the high probability of developing degenerative joint disease.

Patellar Luxation

This is another problem which, like hip and elbow dysplasia, is thought to arise from joint laxity, in this case of the stifle (knee) joint. This condition is thought to be inherited. The patella, or kneecap, normally sits in a groove in the femur at the front of the stifle joint. In dogs with patellar luxation (also called slipped patella), the groove is flattened, and the patella does not stay within the groove but slips out to one side or the other, most often to the inside of the leg (Fig. 6.15). In the past, patellar luxation was thought to be a condition of only smaller dogs, but in recent years, there has been an increase in the number of large and giant breeds with the condition.

A dog with a mild case of patellar luxation will suddenly carry the affected leg for several steps until the patella slips back in, and will then appear

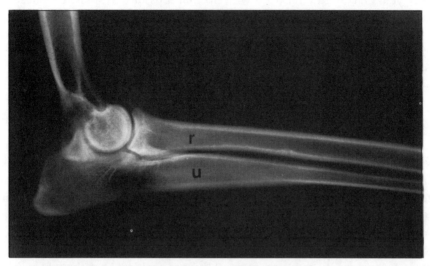

Fig. 6.13. Normal elbow joint: r—radius, u—ulna.

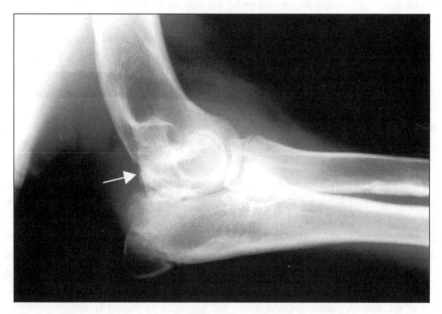

Fig. 6.14. Elbow dysplasia in a German Shepherd Dog. Note the roughened edges that are typical of degenerative joint disease. The arrow indicates a piece of bone that has separated from the ulna (ununited anconeal process).

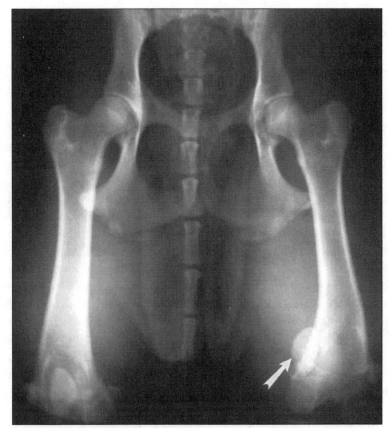

Fig. 6.15. Patellar luxation in a Bull Terrier. The patella on the left is in the correct position within the femoral groove. The patella on the right (arrow) has slipped medially (toward the other leg).

normal again, with no evidence of lameness at all. Many dogs live with intermittent patellar luxation for years, and some have luxated patellas for a lifetime without developing signs of arthritis. But frequently degenerative joint disease develops and begins to impair joint function on a more continuous basis. In severe cases, the patella may be continually luxated. In these dogs, the periods of lameness will be longer, and the leg may actually become deformed, with both the femur and the tibia twisting as they accommodate to the increased stresses placed upon them.

Surgical treatment of patellar luxation is of variable success in returning a performance dog to training and competition. For this reason, it is recommended that only dogs with severe patellar luxation, or luxation that significantly interferes with performance, undergo surgical repair. Surgery involves reconstruction of the bones and/or the soft tissues of the joint so that the patella can be stabilized.

Intervertebral Disk Disease

The spinal cord is surrounded and protected by a row of interlocking bones called the vertebrae. Between each vertebral bone, there is a circular structure called an intervertebral disk, which is made of a very resilient type of connective tissue. This disk forms a bumper to cushion the two vertebrae on either side against concussion. Just as in humans, virtually every dog has one or more intervertebral disks that undergo degeneration over the course of a lifetime. The disks that most commonly degenerate are those of the neck and the lumbar (lower back) spine because these are the areas of the spinal cord that have the most flexibility. Breeds that are most prone to degenerative disk disease are those with long bodies and short legs such as Dachshunds, Corgis, and Peking-ese. However, disk degeneration is also relatively common in other breeds, particularly in dogs that do a lot of hard working and playing. A degenerated disk is not as pliable as a normal disk and, under pressure, a portion of the degenerated disk may get squeezed out into the spinal canal where it presses on the spinal cord. The dog may show sudden or gradual onset of pain, loss of sensation, and various degrees of loss of motor function. Clinical signs may improve for a while and then worsen, depending on the amount of disk material that has penetrated into the spinal canal.

A diagnosis of intervertebral disk disease is made by having a veterinarian or veterinary neurologist perform a neurological examination and take spinal radiographs. If necessary, a myelogram may have to be performed, in which a contrast material is injected to determine whether the spinal cord is being pinched (Fig. 6.16). Conservative treatment of degenerative disk disease consists of strict rest to allow the damaged spinal cord to heal and to prevent the further extrusion of disk material. Analgesics such as aspirin are not recommended because the dog may then worsen the damage by physical activity. Massage and acupuncture can be very helpful in relieving pain and promoting healing. If the problem recurs or the dog is in severe pain, surgical intervention may be necessary. If the damage to the spinal cord has not been too extensive, and if the owner is willing to undertake longterm physical therapy, a dog with degenerative disk disease can performance events again, even jumping in obedience. The owner, however, will always have to be aware of the possibility of re-injury, and ensure that environmental conditions are ideal before competing.

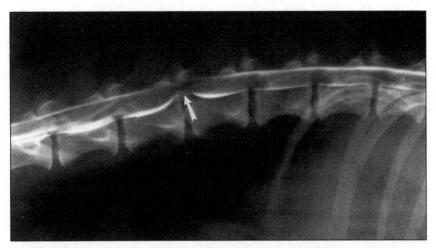

Fig. 6.16. Intervertebral disk disease in a Miniature Dachshund. A contrast material has been injected into the space between the spinal cord and the vertebrae. The contrast material indicates an area (arrow) where the disk is pressing up on the spinal cord.

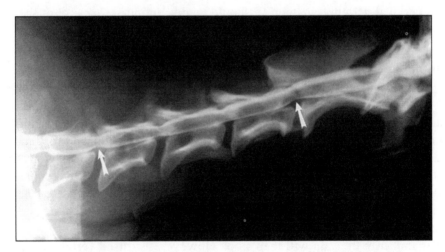

Fig. 6.17. Cervical vertebral instability in a Doberman Pinscher. Contrast material has outlined several areas (arrows) where the bones are pressing on the spinal cord.

Cervical Vertebral Instability

This condition, also known as "wobbler syndrome," is a degenerative disease of the cervical (neck) vertebrae, which occurs in Doberman Pinschers, Great Danes, and other large and giant breeds of dogs. It occurs more frequently in males than females and, as the name suggests, is characterized by a lack of stability of the vertebrae in the neck. The joints between the vertebrae are supposed to have smooth, well-fitted surfaces that allow the bones to flex against each other without moving so much as to press on the spinal cord. In dogs with cervical vertebral instability, the vertebral bones become deformed, particularly in the area where the two bones meet. They then press on the spinal cord, especially when the neck is flexed. The damage to the spinal cord starts gradually, and dogs may not develop clinical signs until they are several months or years old. An affected dog will typically begin to scuff one or both hind legs on the ground when walking and may have trouble pivoting in a tight circle. Eventually the dog will become uncoordinated, and the condition may even progress to the point that the dog has difficulty rising.

Definitive diagnosis of this condition can be made with a complete neurological examination and radiographs of the cervical vertebrae using a radio-opaque material to outline the location of the spinal cord within the spinal canal (Fig. 6.17). Therapy usually consists of preventing further damage by reducing exercise and providing supportive care. Surgical treatment usually does not have a high level of success. The performance career of a dog with clinical cervical vertebral instability should be discontinued, because of the risk of ongoing damage to the spinal cord.

Spondylosis

This is a syndrome in which bony outgrowths or spurs develop on the lower (and sometimes also the upper) parts of the vertebral bones, generally in the lumbar area (Figs. 6.18, 6.19). Bony spurs in this location are seen quite often in middle-aged or older dogs, particularly in large breeds, and the fact that they are present does not mean that the dog will suffer any pain or obvious reduction in function. It is thought that these bony growths form in response to disk degeneration that results in joint laxity. Sometimes the presence of these bony growths can cause pain, especially when the dog is flexing and extending its spine, as during jumping. Eventually the spurs on opposing bones grow together and fuse; the pain will then stop. However, the fused vertebrae lack flexibility, resulting in increased flexion of the adjacent vertebrae, and new spurs may begin to form in those locations.

It can be hard to be certain that the spondylosis is the cause of a dog's back pain. Other causes of back pain, such as intervertebral disk disease or muscle soreness, should also be considered. Generally, treatment is conservative and consists of rest and analgesics. Occasionally, the bony proliferations may be so profuse that they entrap some of the many nerves that exit from the spinal cord. In that case, surgery may be necessary to remove the bony growths.

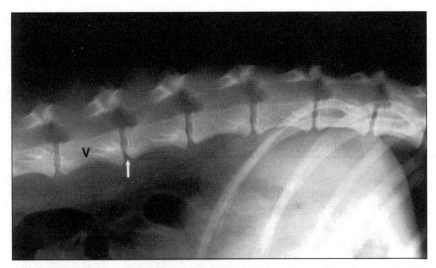

Fig. 6.18. Normal spine: v—vertebral bone. The arrow indicates the space between vertebrae where the intervertebral disk lies.

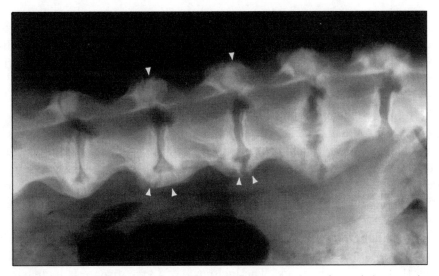

Fig. 6.19. Spondylosis in a Saint Bernard. Bony spurs have formed above and below several of the vertebral bones (arrowheads).

Chiropractic adjustment can be helpful to stop the cycle of pain from nerve entrapment causing further muscle spasms and more pain. Acupuncture can also help alleviate the pain of this condition.

Lyme Disease

Lyme disease is a tick-borne bacterial disease which was first recognized in humans in Lyme, Connecticut in 1975. The first case in a dog was recognized in 1984. The Lyme disease bacterium is carried from white-tailed deer and the white-footed mouse to the dog by the very small deer tick. Other species of ticks have been implicated as well. It is estimated that up to 40% of the deer ticks in endemic areas such as the Northeastern United States may contain the bacterium that causes Lyme disease.

The acute disease in dogs is characterized by sudden onset of hot, swollen joints, lameness, muscle pain, fever, and malaise. Once the Lyme disease bacterium has entered the dog's body, it can remain for life in the connective tissues of joints and other musculoskeletal structures, even after antibiotic treatment. The Lyme disease bacterium can cause severe arthritis in one or several joints and, if left untreated, can cause permanent damage to the joint(s). The way in which the bacterium causes arthritis is not fully understood, but it is thought to be an autoimmune phenomenon in which the body's immune system attacks the joint tissues.

Diagnosis of Lyme disease is made by noting a history of exposure to ticks, recognizing the clinical signs, and testing the dog's serum for antibodies to the bacterium. The acute disease is responsive to administration of appropriate antibiotics, particularly if they are started as soon as possible. Because the disease can become chronic and recurring, some veterinarians recommend that a dog living in an endemic area be started on a course of antibiotics if it has clinical signs of the disease, even though the serum test is negative. This is because the dog's body may take up to two weeks to produce an antibody response to the bacterium, so the test will be negative, even though the dog is acutely infected. A later serum sample can then be taken and tested again to confirm the diagnosis.

It is thought that many dogs have a natural immunity to the bacterium, because the number of dogs that develop the disease is small compared to the number that are bitten by ticks. The incidence of Lyme disease is increasing steadily across the United States and Canada, and any dog with sudden joint pain should be tested for Lyme disease. In the past, vaccination for Lyme disease was recommended for all dogs in endemic areas and for dogs that frequently trained and competed outdoors (dogs in field trials, hunting tests, herding tests, etc.). However, the vaccine made from whole bacteria has been associated with acute, fatal kidney disease in a number of breeds of dogs, especially Labrador Retrievers, Shetland Sheepdogs, and Golden Retrievers. At this writing, there is a new,

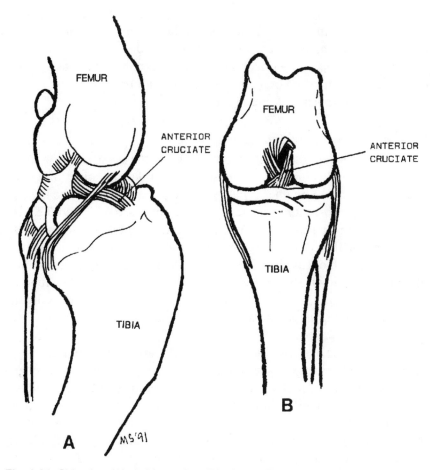

Fig. 6.20. Side view (A) and front view (B) of the stifle joint, showing the location of the anterior cruciate ligament as it crosses the joint space from the back of the femur to the front of the tibia.

recombinant subunit vaccine available that may be safer than the whole bacteria vaccine. If you live in an endemic area and your dog is regularly exposed to ticks, the best defense against Lyme disease is to use a topical product that repels ticks, thereby preventing exposure to the bacterium in the first place.

COMMON CAUSES OF LAMENESS - LIGAMENTS & TENDONS

Injuries to ligaments and tendons are very common in performance dogs. A stretch injury to a ligament is called a sprain, whereas a stretch injury to the muscle and/or tendon is a strain. Ligaments and tendons have great tensile strength, but are very inelastic. If the load on the ligament or tendon is greater than its tensile strength, damage occurs, with the tissue stretching and some or all of its fibers breaking. The fibers then heal by forming scar tissue, which has neither elasticity nor tensile strength. Repeated small tears to a tendon or ligament can therefore leave it more susceptible to rupture.

Rupture of the Anterior Cruciate Ligament

Anterior cruciate ligament rupture is one of the most common injuries in performance dogs and is the most common cause of degenerative joint disease of the stifle. There are two ligaments that run across the middle of the knee joint: the anterior and the posterior cruciate ligaments (Fig. 6.20). When the stifle is stressed, generally by a forced overextension of the joint or a sudden twisting of the knee when it is flexed, these ligaments, the anterior cruciate ligament in particular, can stretch or rupture. These injuries are relatively common in dogs participating in hunting tests and field trials, herding tests, lure coursing, and agility. One of the most common ways in which the anterior cruciate ligament is damaged is when a dog steps into a hole while running.

Rupture of the anterior cruciate ligament causes the knee joint to become loose, and this predisposes it to other injury. The most common is damage to the meniscus, a small, crescent-shaped piece of cartilage that forms a cushion between the two main bones that form the joint. Damage to the meniscus occurs in approximately 50 percent of dogs with ruptured cruciate ligaments and can contribute significantly to the pain of the injury. In addition, the joint laxity and abnormal stress predisposes the joint to degenerative joint disease. Dogs that are overweight are particularly susceptible to anterior cruciate ligament rupture, and the dog's excess weight places extra stress on the ligament after it has been surgically repaired, thereby slowing the healing process. A surprisingly high percentage of dogs with anterior cruciate ligament rupture in one knee go on to rupture the other anterior cruciate ligament. Whether this is because of genetic susceptibility, subclinical damage to the second leg from the same causes as the first leg, the added stress on the normal leg while the injured one is healing, or a combination of these factors is not known. Regardless, this injury can be heart-breaking for owner and canine teammate alike.

The first sign of damage to the anterior cruciate ligament is often when the dog begins to carry one of its back legs rather than bearing weight on it. After a few days, the dog will gradually put more and more weight on the affected leg. If given crate rest, the dog may appear to get better. He may then perform with only occasional limping, or even none at all. But this improvement can be deceptive. The muscles of the rear leg can hold the knee joint together enough for the dog to function, but the joint remains much looser than normal, and degenerative joint disease begins to develop. For this reason, although crate rest may be a suitable treatment for a stay-at-home companion dog, surgical repair should be given serious consideration for a dog that will be expected to perform for years to come. Surgery should be performed as soon as possible because the ligament, if completely ruptured, cannot repair itself. There are many different surgical techniques used, based on the dog's size and the degree of damage. A performance dog with a repaired anterior cruciate ligament will always be susceptible to re-injury and may develop degenerative joint disease earlier than if the injury had never occurred. However, surgical repair, preferably by a surgeon who understands the demands placed on a performance dog, will give the dog the best chance of living a pain-free life and of returning to its former level of activity.

Sprain

One of the most common ligamentous injuries in performance dogs is sprain of the carpal (wrist) joint. This can occur when a dog falls from a height or when the foot twists on uneven ground while running. Carpal sprain is caused by hyperextension or hyperflexion of the limb, which stretches or tears the ligaments that hold the joint together. The bones of the carpus may also become dislocated. Sprains as a result of hyperextension can also happen in other joints, but most often occur in the tarsus (hock), the stifle, the elbow, and the joints of the toes.

A dog with a sprain will become suddenly lame and will not bear weight on the leg. There will usually be swelling and heat in the joint area. In the case of an acute injury, the owner can prevent further damage to the tissues and significantly hasten repair by applying ice packs to the affected limb immediately. A dog with a serious sprain should be taken to a veterinarian for a thorough workup to be sure that there are no fractured bones. Treatment of mild sprains involves forced rest for seven to ten days, followed by a similar period of light activity, and then a gradual return to full function. Dogs with more severe sprains may need to have the leg splinted, and full function may not be regained for several months after the injury. If ligaments have been ruptured by the trauma, surgery may be necessary to avoid permanent joint laxity and resultant degenerative joint disease.

Strain

The most common strains in performance dogs involves the biceps or supraspinatus tendons, those that aid in extension of the shoulder joint. This

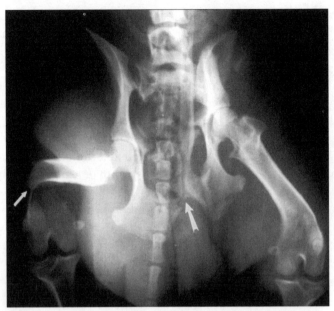

Fig. 6.21. Pelvic radiograph of a Pembroke Welsh Corgi that was hit by a car. There are fractures of the femur (small arrow) and pelvis (large arrow). Pieces of both the femur and the pelvis are displaced from their normal positions, requiring surgery to reset. Note the bend in the intact femur. This is normal in chondrodysplastic breeds.

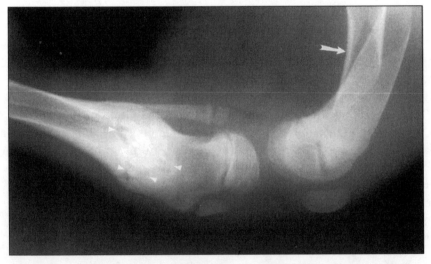

Fig. 6.22. A healing fracture in the tibia of a mixed breed dog. There is a swelling (callus) in the area where the fracture is healing (arrowheads). There is also a femoral fracture (arrow) which has not begun to heal because the fractured ends are not in apposition to each other.

injury is relatively common in middle-aged dogs of large breeds and is more common in poorly conditioned dogs. Lameness in these dogs may be only mild or intermittent and occurs when the dog flexes and extends the leg. This impairs the ability of the dog to swing its leg forward, so this part of the stride is short-ened.

Treatment of muscle strain involves rest for four to six weeks, ice packs, massage, and anti-inflammatory drug therapy. Premature return to activity can result in re-injury and may cause the development of scar tissue in the muscle which, because of its inability to stretch, can impair function permanently.

COMMON CAUSES OF LAMENESS - BONES

Fractures

A fracture is a partial or complete break in the continuity of the bone. Fractures are classified by severity; these classifications are the same for dogs and people. The least serious type of fracture is the greenstick fracture, in which one side of the bone is broken but other side is just bent, so that the two ends of the bones are not displaced from their original positions. This type of partial fracture is often seen in young, growing dogs because their bones are less brittle than those of adults. A complete fracture is one in which the bone is broken through its width. Generally, the pieces of bone are displaced in a complete fracture because contractions of the muscle move the broken pieces of bone away from their original location (Figure 6.21). A complete fracture is more serious than a greenstick fracture because the damage to the bone is greater and there is usually damage to the surrounding muscles and perhaps ligaments and tendons. Complete fractures can be simple, in which there are just two pieces of bone, or comminuted, in which there are many pieces of bone which have to be replaced to their original location before correct healing can begin.

Despite the fact that it seems solid and inflexible, bone is a living tissue made up of living cells, like any other tissue in the body. When a bone breaks, a blood clot forms at the break. Cells from the blood immediately move in to begin the repair process (Fig. 6.22). These cells secrete many substances that induce various cells to replicate and new tissue to form. As the bone heals, the inflammation decreases, and the bone reshapes itself into its original form.

Treatment of fractures involves setting the pieces of bones as close to their original position as possible. This hastens the healing process by reducing the amount of reshaping that the bone must undergo. When a fracture involves a joint surface, it is essential that the bones are set in as close to their original

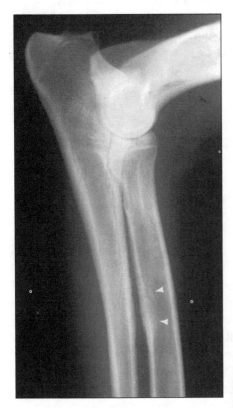

Fig. 6.23. Panosteitis in a German Shepherd Dog. There are multiple small areas of increased density within the bone (arrowheads).

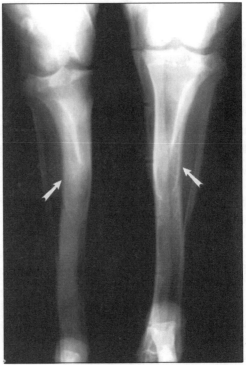

Fig. 6.24. Congenital deformity (valgus deformity) of the tibial bones of a German Shepherd Dog. The bones are bent inward (arrows) a little way below the stifle joints.

position as possible to minimize irregularities in the joint surface that would cause abnormal wear and thus hasten the onset of degenerative joint disease. Because bones begin to heal immediately, treatment of fractures should occur as soon after the break as the patient's condition permits. Fractures can be repaired externally using a splint, a cast, or an external fixator (pins inserted in the leg and connected by external bars) on the leg to hold the bones together. Internal fixation involves surgery and the use of wires, pins, screws, and/or plates to hold the bones securely in place. One method of repair (external or internal) is not necessarily better than the other. The optimal method depends on the type of break, the size, age, and health of the dog, and the abilities and expertise of the attending veterinarian.

After the bones have been set, the dog should be examined twice daily for signs of discomfort. These signs include swelling, an increase in the temperature of the foot, a foul odor, chewing on the leg or cast, fever, depression, or reduced appetite. A dog showing any of these signs should receive prompt veterinary attention.

Panosteitis

This is a bone condition of unknown cause. It tends to occur in the same breeds of dogs that have a high incidence of elbow dysplasia, hip dysplasia, and osteochondrosis, and is especially common in German Shepherd Dogs and in Doberman Pinschers. It is uncommon for panosteitis to occur in a dog over two years of age, although it can affect dogs up to five years of age.

An affected dog will suddenly become lame with no history of trauma. The lameness may continue intermittently in one leg, then occur several weeks later in another. When radiographs are taken, areas of increased density can be seen in the bone (Fig. 6.23). These represent areas of inflammation within the bone marrow cavity. The prognosis for this condition is excellent, and it usually clears up in several weeks or months without specific treatment. Supportive treatment consists of analgesics and rest with moderate exercise. Anti-inflammatory drugs also are sometimes helpful.

Limb Deformity

Limb deformities are relatively common in dogs, just as they are in people. They may be hereditary, they may develop in a dog which has had an injury to the growth plate, causing one side of the growth plate to close while the other side continues to grow and lengthen the bone, or they may develop as a result of nutritional imbalances. Any of the long bones can be affected, but limb deformities are most common in the tibia (Fig. 6.24) and femur of the rear leg, and the radius in the front leg. Depending on the severity of the condition, limb deformity may significantly impair performance.

COMMON CAUSES OF LAMENESS - MUSCLE

Muscle Soreness

There are two kinds of muscle soreness that are described in human athletes: soreness that occurs during and immediately after exercise, and delayed soreness that occurs two to four days after exertion. We can assume that dogs suffer from the same types of soreness, although they do not often tell us. The causes of these types of soreness are complex and not completely understood, but may include damage to muscle fibers or nerves or interference with the blood supply. Dogs suffering from muscle soreness will appear stiff when arising. They may be lame immediately after rest, but not after moving around for a while. Animals that appear to be suffering from soreness should be rested for a day or two and then placed on a reduced training schedule for several days to allow time for the muscles to heal. Muscle soreness can be prevented by providing the dog with an adequate warm-up before training or competing and by increasing the intensity and frequency of training gradually.

Muscle Trauma

Trauma can affect any of the muscles in the body, but the most commonly injured muscles are those that attach the shoulder blade to the body. Unlike the rear leg, which is attached to the body by a sturdy joint (the hip joint), the front leg is attached to the body only by muscles. This muscle can be damaged when the front leg is forcibly pulled away from the body. This can happen if a dog falls with its front leg outstretched, or if it bangs the shoulder into a solid object during a performance event. A dog with injury to this muscle will be very sore and will favor the leg. Treatment consists of rest, gentle massage, and a gradual increase in exercise.

CONDITIONS OF THE NERVOUS SYSTEM

Spinal Cord Trauma

Spinal cord trauma in performance dogs is most commonly caused by running into stationary objects or by falling (for example, slipping when landing from the broad jump in obedience). Such an accident can cause a degenerated disk to protrude, or one of the vertebral bones to fracture and press on the spinal cord. The clinical signs are similar to those for intervertebral disk disease, but there is usually a history of trauma.

Traumatic Peripheral Neuropathy

Damage to one or more peripheral nerves is a relatively common finding secondary to trauma. Many of the nerves in the legs run just underneath the skin and thus are quite susceptible to damage. Severe nerve injury can occur when the front leg is pulled away from the body, causing damage to the nerves that serve the arm. This may happen when a dog's leg falls in an unseen groundhog hole or when a front leg slips out from under the dog as it tries to turn immediately upon landing from a jump. A nerve that has been traumatized will lose part or all of its function, depending on the degree of damage. If the damage has not been too severe, the nerve will gradually repair itself over weeks or months and will begin to function again. If the trauma has been very severe, the nerve may not ever regain full function. During the time that the nerve is regenerating, the muscle(s) that it serves will atrophy (become smaller) because of disuse. Sometimes nerve damage is first diagnosed because the muscles on one side of the leg are smaller than those on the other side. Gradually, as the nerve repairs itself, muscle use increases, and the muscle regains its normal size and shape.

NUTRITIONAL DISORDERS

There are three main nutritional disorders in dogs that can affect the bones and joints: 1) obesity, 2) the effects of feeding an all-meat diet, and 3) oversupplementation in large and giant breeds of dogs. Bones and joints continuously undergo wear and tear due to the mechanical forces of motion within joints. In overweight dogs, there is more stress placed on the bones and joints and their supporting structures. Over years of use or overuse, this can gradually lead to the development of degenerative joint disease.

Dogs fed diets of only organ meats do not ingest enough calcium for proper development of bones and joints. Organ meats are low in calcium and high in phosphorus; this dietary imbalance will cause the body to resorb mineral from the bones to maintain the correct blood calcium level. Calcium loss causes the bones to become thin and weak. Carnivores fed strictly organ meats may have multiple fractures. When radiographed, the bones will appear thin and almost translucent (Fig. 6.25). The bones may have so little calcium that they can bend like rubber.

Most commercial dog foods contain the proper quantities of calcium and phosphorus. Sometimes people owning large or giant breeds of dogs believe that it is necessary to add calcium or bone meal to their dogs' diets. This can lead to a severe dietary imbalance. Young Great Danes experimentally fed an over-supplemented diet had accelerated bone growth, flat feet, badly turned-out

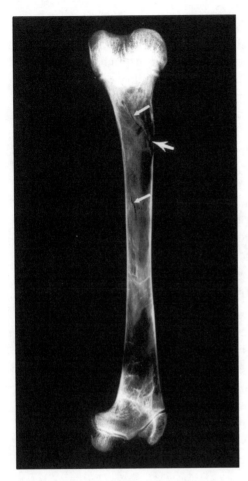

Fig. 6.25. Nutritional bone disease in a lynx. This animal was fed only organ meats and developed lameness so severe that it had to be euthanized. The bone is very thin (large arrow) and has several greenstick fractures (small arrows).

forepaws, cowhocked rear limbs, joint enlargement, and arched backs. Their littermates fed regulated amounts of a balanced dog food with no supplementation had none of these problems. Rapid growth is also associated with an increased incidence of hip dysplasia, osteochondrosis (cartilage degeneration), and other bone and joint problems. It should be evident, therefore, that rapid bone growth is not desirable. It is better to allow the dog to grow at a reasonable rate — he will reach the same size eventually and will be healthier for it.

FIRST AID FOR SPORTS INJURIES

When injuries occur in performance events, there is often no veterinarian close by. Clubs holding performance events should have a first aid kit available (Table 6.4) and at least one member present who is well-versed in basic first aid. A knowledge of canine first aid can help you lessen the severity of injury and perhaps save your dog's life. The first thing you must do when your dog has

Table 6.4
Suggested Contents for a First Aid Kit

Waterproof container

Adhesive tape	Gauze (roll)
Alcohol swabs	Green soap (30 cc.)
Aspirin 325 mg.	Kling bandage
(enteric coated)	Loperamide (antidiarrheal)
Athlete's foot powder	Lubricating jelly
Bacitracin	Peroxide (30 cc.)
Cohesive bandage	Razor blade (covered)
Cold pack	Saline solution (30 cc.)
Cotton squares	Stockingette
Cotton swabs	Syringe (5 cc.)
Diphenhydramine 25 mg.	Thermometer (rectal)
(e.g., Benedryl®)	Tweezers (flat-ended)

injured itself is to remove it from competition. This may seem self-evident, but I have been in the position where my dog was obviously limping and the judge either did not notice or chose to ignore it rather than excuse my dog. It was up to me to request to be excused from competition.

The next step is to observe the dog carefully. If the dog is limping, the legs should be examined carefully. Any areas of swelling should be wrapped in ice packs. Cuts should be treated by applying pressure to stop the bleeding, then wrapping the leg in clean gauze for a trip to the veterinarian. Cuts that require sutures should be examined by a veterinarian immediately. If a cut is more than about six hours old, it should not be sutured because it is almost certainly contaminated with bacteria from the environment. Suturing the cut would just trap the bacteria within the wound, resulting in infection and possibly increased scarring. An older cut should be thoroughly cleaned and allowed to heal gradually as an open wound.

If a limb is broken, and a veterinary clinic is close by, carefully place the dog on a firm, level surface and take it to the clinic. If you are far from veterinary help, the leg should be carefully splinted before the dog is moved. The best splint is something that is rigid but padded, such as a board wrapped with a towel. The splint should be placed against the dog's limb, avoiding movement of the bones as much as possible. The leg and the joints above and below the break should be taped to the splint. The dog should then be transported to a veterinary clinic.

Most injuries suffered during canine performance events are to the legs, but in some sports, a dog can sustain injury to its head, spine, chest, or abdomen. In the case of such an injury, the dog should be given a quick examination. The degree of consciousness should be assessed by observing the dog's responses to its environment. The dog should respond when called by name and should be able to follow your hand with its eyes. The gums should be wet and pink. When pressed, they should turn momentarily white and then become pink again as the capillaries refill. If the dog is in shock, which may happen if the dog is bleeding internally, it will have clammy gums that are pale and do not regain their color rapidly after being pressed. The dog should also be observed for abnormalities in respiration. Most dogs have a resting respiratory rate of between 10 and 30 breaths per minute, which increases during and immediately after exercise. In addition, the pulse should be taken by pressing on the femoral artery located on the inside of the leg, just where it joins the body. During your next trip to the veterinarian, ask her to show you how to feel your dog's pulse at this site. The pulse should feel strong and regular. The normal heart rate of dogs ranges from 60 to 160 beats per minute and varies with body size; the smaller the dog, the more rapid the pulse. If the dog shows any sign of change in consciousness, difficulty in standing, abnormalities in breathing, or a weak pulse, it should be placed on its side on a firm surface and kept calm until it can be seen by a veterinarian.

There are many physical conditions capable of affecting performance. Observant handling from puppyhood on will help detect these as early as possible.

Marcia Halliday

7.

PROBLEMS THAT

AFFECT PERFORMANCE

A dog can't get struck by lightning. You know why?
'Cause he's too close to the ground. See, lightning
strikes tall things. Now, if they were giraffes out there
in that field, now then we'd be in trouble. But you
sure don't have to worry about dogs.
Don Knotts on "The Andy Griffith Show"

There are many structural and medical conditions that can affect performance. Quite a few of these problems are a result of breeding programs designed to produce dogs with certain physical characteristics. The shortened muzzles of the brachycephalic breeds, which can impair breathing, and the narrow, deep chests of breeds such as the Doberman Pinscher and the Borzoi, which increase their susceptibility to gastric torsion are the result of deliberate selection of these traits in breeding programs. In addition, there are hundreds of known hereditary diseases in dogs, and the number continues to rise. Due to the doubling up of similar genetic information, genetic problems are more common in purebred dogs than in random-bred dogs. The most common hereditary problems involve the musculoskeletal system, the nervous system, and the cardiovascular system — coincidentally, the same systems that are so important in performance. This chapter outlines some of the causes, clinical signs, and treatment options for the most common medical and genetic conditions that affect performance.

CONDITIONS OF THE EYES

Collie Eye Anomaly

Ocular problems are common in breeds with long, narrow skulls. These dogs have been bred to have a narrowed zygomatic arch — the cheekbone that holds the eye in place in the bony orbit of the skull. In some cases, this narrowing has caused a series of secondary defects of the eye, some of which can seriously affect vision. The best example of this is Collie Eye Anomaly. In this condition, the eyeball has become wrinkled so that it can fit into the smaller bony orbit. The wrinkling prevents adequate focusing of the visual image on the retina at the back of the eye. In affected dogs, large areas of the visual field may be out of focus. Only a few years ago, it was estimated that 75% of all Collies suffered from Collie Eye Anomaly. In an effort to eradicate this problem from their breed, reputable breeders now have all breeding stock examined for the presence of Collie Eye Anomaly and do not breed affected animals.

Entropion

Entropion is an inversion of the eyelid, seen most commonly in breeds such as Chow Chows and Chinese Shar-Pei that have wide skulls and sunken eyes, or excessive folds of the skin of the face. In these dogs, the eyelids are rolled inward, and the hairs on the eyelids rub on the cornea, causing irritation and damage. This condition is very painful to the dog and must be corrected surgically or blindness may result. Dogs cannot be shown in conformation after surgical correction for entropion, and these dogs should not be bred since the condition is an inherited defect affecting facial structure.

Progressive Retinal Atrophy

Progressive retinal atrophy (PRA) is a group of genetically recessive conditions that affect a number of breeds. In PRA, the photoreceptors (cells that collect and process visual information) degenerate, causing first night blindness and ultimately total blindness. In some breeds, such as Irish Setters, the age of onset is 4 to 6 months. In other breeds, such as Miniature Poodles, the condition begins at 3 to 5 years. Recent progress in mapping the canine genome has made tests for PRA in Irish Setters and some other breeds possible. It is hoped that, with testing and selective breeding, this condition will be eliminated.

Another kind of PRA, central PRA (CPRA), occurs in several breeds, including Labrador and Golden Retrievers, Collies, Shetland Sheepdogs, and other breeds. This is inherited as a dominant trait with variable penetrance — additional genes modify the severity of disease. Dogs with this condition have progressive deterioration of their vision over several years. There is no treatment for either form of PRA.

Cataracts

Cataract is a general term denoting an opacity of the lens. Cataracts may be genetic in origin or may occur secondary to inflammation or systemic disease, such as diabetes mellitus. The genetic form may develop in the first few months of life or during middle age. An ophthalmological examination is usually necessary to make a diagnosis. Depending on their size and location in the lens, cataracts may significantly interfere with vision. Cataracts should not be mistaken for the bluing of the lens that occurs in most older dogs as the lenses harden. This lenticular sclerosis is often mistakenly referred to as cataracts. Lenticular sclerosis does not cause blindness, but dogs with the condition have difficulty focusing on objects up close, a predicament familiar to most humans over the age of 45 years!

CONDITIONS OF THE EARS

Otitis

Otitis (ear infection) is very common in dogs. About 80 percent of the cases are in dogs with dropped ears. Factors such as high humidity or moisture in the ears from swimming can soak the skin of the ear canal, reducing its normal protective ability. Bacteria and fungi that normally live on the surface of the skin then penetrate and cause infection and inflammation. Initially, otitis may involve only the outer ear, but if unchecked it may move to the middle and inner ear, interfering with hearing and balance. A routine weekly check of the ears for abnormal discharge or smell is an important preventive measure against ear infections.

Deafness

Congenital (present at birth) deafness is seen most commonly in double merle (white appearing due to a lack of primary color) dogs that are the result of a breeding in which both parents have merle (black and gray spotted or red and gray spotted) coats. This coloring is most commonly seen in Shetland Sheepdogs (Fig. 7.1) and Australian Shepherds. Other breeds in which congenital deafness occurs include Dalmatians, Old English Sheepdogs, Cocker Spaniels, and Bull Terriers. Acquired deafness, caused by deterioration of the structures within the middle and inner ear, is very common in older dogs, especially those over ten years of age. Older dogs first lose their ability to hear deeper sounds, then high-pitched sounds.

Fig. 7.1. A blue merle Shetland Sheepdog performing in agility.

CONDITIONS OF THE TEETH

Abnormal Bite

There are three main abnormalities of bite: overshot bite, undershot bite, and wry mouth. In some breeds, particularly those that require a scissors bite, an undershot jaw, in which the lower jaw protrudes in front of the upper, is considered a serious fault and will likely prevent such a dog from being competitive in the breed ring (Fig. 7.2). An overshot jaw, or overbite, in which the upper incisors protrude too far (sometimes more than a half inch) in front of the lower, is another serious abnormality of bite (Fig. 7.3). An overshot or undershot jaw can prevent a dog from grasping objects properly in its mouth and probably also affects the dog's ability to chew. A third abnormality of bite is called wry mouth. This problem develops because one side of the jaw grows faster than the other. The result is that the lower jaw doesn't meet the upper jaw evenly on both sides of the mouth, so that one side of the jaw may have a scissors bite while the other side is undershot (Fig. 7.4). As a result, the teeth do not act in concert for grasping and chewing.

Misalignment and Malocclusion

Just as in humans, dogs may have misaligned teeth, in which the incisors are not lined up in an even row next to each other. Brachycephalic dogs commonly have misaligned teeth, since the shortening of the muzzle causes the teeth

Fig. 7.2. Undershot bite. The lower incisor teeth protrude beyond the upper incisors. (From: Schlehr, *Golden Retriever*)

Fig. 7.3. Overshot bite. The upper incisor teeth protrude too far past the lower incisors. (From: Schlehr, *Golden Retriever*)

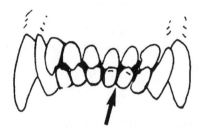

Fig. 7.4. Wry mouth. Because the two sides of the jaw have grown to different lengths, the incisors are undershot on the left side (arrow) and form a scissors bite on the right side of the dog's mouth. (From: Schlehr, *Golden Retriever*)

to be crowded together. Except in severe cases, misalignment of only the incisors doesn't affect the dog's ability to eat or perform.

Malocclusion is a condition in which the upper molar teeth do not mesh with the lower teeth properly. This is more serious than misalignment because it prevents the dog from shutting its mouth completely, and thus may interfere with chewing. The use of orthodontics to correct bite abnormalities, misalignment, and/or malocclusion for the purpose of allowing an animal to conform to breed specifications is unethical.

Fractured Teeth

It is relatively common for dogs to have fractured teeth. One study found fractured teeth in 27 percent of the dogs examined. Fractures generally occur as a result of catching or chewing on stones or other hard objects. Many retrievers are inveterate rock hounds, hunting for rocks on the bottoms of ponds and carrying them everywhere. These dogs' teeth may be worn to the gum from this apparently pleasurable activity. Surprisingly, dogs with cracked or fractured teeth frequently do not show evidence of pain unless the fracture extends deep enough to involve the nerve. However, a fracture or crack in a tooth provides a niche for bacteria to grow. This can eventually result in abscessation (deep infection) of the tooth. This condition is painful, and an affected dog may be unwilling to retrieve certain objects or to hold metal objects in its mouth. An abscessed tooth should be treated with appropriate antibiotics and repaired or extracted.

Retained Deciduous Teeth

This is a very common condition in which the baby teeth do not fall out when the adult teeth are erupting. The incisor and canine teeth are the most commonly affected. Retained puppy teeth should be extracted as soon as possible because they may cause misalignment of the teeth, and they will also form a focus for the development of plaque and calculus.

Extra Teeth

Extra teeth are quite common, especially in Sporting and Hound breeds. Usually the extra teeth are premolars. These extra teeth should be removed only if there is crowding of the teeth or if periodontal disease develops.

Missing Teeth

Dogs may be missing one or more molars or premolars as adults. For a Sporting Dog that is expected to carry upland game using its premolars and molars, missing teeth is a serious fault. This is almost certainly a hereditary condition because it is carried from generation to generation in certain lines of dogs of a variety of breeds. To prevent the fault from becoming common, some breeds are required to have full dentition to complete the championship title.

Dental Caries

Dental caries (cavities) are uncommon in dogs for several reasons: they have less sugar in their diets, their saliva neutralizes oral acids, and dogs' teeth do not have pits that retain food particles. With age, a dog's teeth do eventually wear down, particularly the incisors and canines. Tooth wear can be accelerated by some dogs' favorite activities, such as disc catching and rock retrieving. If the wearing occurs slowly, the tooth will undergo repair to cover up the pulp cavity. The repaired area can be seen as a brown spot on the top of the tooth, often mistaken for a cavity.

CONDITIONS AFFECTING SCENTING

There are many medical conditions that can impair a dog's scenting ability, either temporarily or permanently. Kennel cough, sinus infections, and upper respiratory tract infections can all cause inflammation of the tissues of the nasal cavity and may temporarily impair the function of the cells responsible for detecting scent. We all have experience with the loss of smell that accompanies the common cold, the human correlate of kennel cough. The most serious canine respiratory infection is distemper, and this can permanently damage a dog's sense of smell. Gingivitis and infections involving the mouth and throat can also decrease scenting ability in dogs.

A number of systemic conditions can impair scenting ability in some dogs. These include diabetes mellitus, hypothyroidism, Cushing's syndrome (the production of too many adrenal steroids), severe renal disease, and estrus. Since scenting ability involves the participation of structures in the brain that recognize and identify odors, conditions such as head trauma and brain tumors can also affect the detection of odors.

A number of drugs are known or thought to affect a dog's ability to scent. Perhaps the best known of these are the glucocorticoids, such as cortisone or prednisone. Some antibiotics and other drugs have also been reported to affect scenting in some dogs. If your dog's scenting ability seems to have deserted him suddenly, consider the possibility of hormonal or drug-induced effects before you blame it on disobedience or a lack of concentration (Fig. 7.5).

CONDITIONS OF THE SKIN AND COAT

Inhalant Allergy

The most common kind of allergy in dogs is atopy — an allergy to inhaled proteins, similar to hay fever in humans. Unlike humans, who respond to pollens with itchy eyes and runny noses, dogs develop itchy skin, particularly the skin of the feet, face, ears, and belly. Dogs may have inhalant allergies seasonally or throughout the year. Many breeds seem to be susceptible to allergies, but the incidence is especially high in West Highland White, Cairn, Scottish, and other harsh-coated terriers, Dalmatians, Shetland Sheepdogs, and Golden and Labrador Retrievers. Intense scratching may result in raw, bleeding skin and makes the skin susceptible to secondary bacterial infection. Experiments have shown that the itch threshold is lower during times of stress, at night, with increased skin temperature, and with decreased skin hydration. The itch-scratch cycle continues because damage to the skin further lowers the itch threshold.

The best way to definitively diagnose inhalant allergies is to perform skin tests, just as is done in people. A dog can be tested for 60 or more different

Fig. 7.5. Hunting dogs like this Flat-Coated Retriever need a good sense of smell to locate fallen game.

Fig. 7.6. An example of a dog with a healthy, glossy coat.

allergens. An area of the skin is shaved, and a tiny amount of the test substance is injected under the skin. The area is then observed to see if a wheal (bump) forms, indicating that a local allergic reaction has taken place. Such tests can be of great benefit, because once the offending allergen is identified, it may be possible to reduce the dog's exposure to that allergen (Fig. 7.6).

Often, however, treatment of allergies in dogs is frustrating. Even if the allergen is identified through skin testing, it may be very difficult to avoid exposure to the allergen, because many dogs are allergic to common, everyday substances such as house dust or grass. Desensitizing injections (allergy shots) help about 75 percent of dogs with inhalant allergies. If these treatments fail, and the itching is bad enough, a short course (1 week) of corticosteroids may be used to stop the itch-scratch cycle. If the signs persist and are severe, the dog may have to be on steroids for a longer time. In this case, the steroids should be given every other day to reduce the considerable side-effects that accompany their use. Long-term use of steroids for treatment of allergies should be considered only when all alternatives have failed. Antihistamines are commonly prescribed and appear to be effective in a small percentage of dogs.

Flea Allergy

The clinical signs of this condition are similar to those of inhalant allergies. In this case, the offending allergen is a protein present in the saliva of fleas, which is intensely irritating to some dogs. With constant exposure, the allergy may become so severe that a single flea bite will cause the dog to chew at itself so much that it loses its hair and develops thick, crusty skin, especially on the feet, at the base of the tail, and around the back legs. You may not actually find fleas on the dog, because fleas spend much of their life cycle in the environment (carpets and furniture are favorite places). There may be only a hint that a flea has been there such as the presence of flea dirt — clumps of dark brown particulate matter (flea feces). Unfortunately, desensitization shots are frequently ineffective in the treatment of flea allergy. Treatment of flea allergy is a three-step process. The fleas must be removed entirely from the dog's environment by bathing the dog with an insecticidal shampoo (or having it dipped in an insecticide), vacuuming (and throwing the vacuum bag away), washing the dog's bedding, and using insecticides to treat the house, the car, the yard, and any other place the dog frequents. After the fleas have been banished, the dog should be put on an oral or topical flea preventive. Many products are available that require only once-a-month treatment. The dog may also need supportive treatment for a while, such as soothing baths or even a short course of steroids.

Color Mutant Alopecia

Fawn and blue Doberman Pinschers (dilutions of the red and black colors, respectively) may carry a gene for a skin disease that causes affected dogs to lose their hair. The hair loss is usually patchy, but in some dogs, it involves all of the hair of the chest and abdomen and can affect the functioning of the skin. Diagnosis of the condition is made by performing a skin biopsy. There is no cure for this condition. Color mutant alopecia has also been diagnosed in red and black Doberman Pinschers that have fawn or blue ancestors.

CONDITIONS OF THE CARDIOVASCULAR SYSTEM

The heart is a very complex organ, and there are many stages in its development at which errors can occur, resulting in congenital defects. Congenital heart defects are three times more common in purebred dogs than in mixed breeds, suggesting that there is a hereditary basis for many of these conditions. There are also many serious conditions of the heart, such as cardiomyopathy and congestive heart failure, that develop in mature dogs. Some of the more common cardiac conditions that affect dogs in their prime are discussed below.

Cardiomyopathy

This is the most common disease of the heart in dogs. The cause of the problem is not known, but it is thought that cardiomyopathy can result from injury to the heart by metabolic, toxic, or infectious agents. The disease is more common in certain breeds and in certain lines within those breeds, but there is no definitive proof of heritability as yet. The disease is relatively common in Doberman Pinschers and Irish Wolfhounds, as well as in several other large and giant breeds. It affects males more frequently than females.

In dogs with cardiomyopathy, the heart muscle cells gradually die, and the heart slowly loses its ability to pump blood throughout the body. The dog then begins to suffer congestive heart failure. The first signs of heart failure include difficulty breathing (especially when the dog is lying down), coughing, and reduced exercise tolerance. A dog with congestive heart failure cannot participate in performance events. It may live for a year or longer with supportive therapy, depending on the severity of the problem when it was diagnosed and the speed with which the condition progresses.

Sub-Aortic Stenosis (SAS)

This malformation involving the aortic valve is especially important in performance dogs because a dog with severe, undiagnosed sub-aortic stenosis can appear healthy but then faint, and sometimes die suddenly, while exercising.

SAS is most common in larger breeds of dogs, and with new technology, such as ultrasound with color Doppler, it is being diagnosed with increasing frequency. SAS has been studied most extensively in the Newfoundland, but it occurs in many other breeds of dogs, including Boxers, German Shepherd Dogs, Golden Retrievers, and others. Its mode of inheritance is most likely autosomal dominant (i.e., the gene is not on one of the sex chromosomes, and therefore can be passed with equal frequency to males or females). In addition, there are probably other genes that modify the degree of severity of the disease.

In dogs with SAS, there is a blockage in the path of the oxygenated blood as it leaves the heart and enters the aorta, the main arterial trunk which delivers blood to the entire body. This blockage causes the heart to work harder to pump the blood. If the blockage is severe, the dog may slowly develop heart failure or it may suddenly die during or after strenuous exercise. Dogs with only a minimal malformation may lead completely normal lives.

A diagnosis of SAS can only be made by a veterinary cardiologist, as it requires sophisticated equipment and experience. The cardiologist will first use a stethoscope to listen for a heart murmur, an abnormality in the sound of the blood as it flows through the heart. If a murmur is heard, it does not mean that the dog has SAS, or even any other cardiac abnormality, because some murmurs are considered "innocent" or not indicative of disease. Further testing is necessary for a definitive diagnosis and to evaluate the severity of the condition. An electrocardiogram and ultrasound evaluation, preferably with color Doppler, which measures the pressure of the blood as it leaves the heart and enters the aorta, will confirm the presence of SAS. Puppies can be tested for SAS, but even if they are declared clear of SAS at the age of a year, SAS may still be diagnosed later. This is a particularly disheartening aspect of this disease. It is recommended that puppies of breeds in which this genetic condition is known to occur be tested before they go to their new homes.

Heartworm

This disease is being diagnosed with increasing frequency in the United States and Canada. The infection rate in dogs not receiving preventive can be greater than 50 percent in areas within 100 miles of the Atlantic coast from Texas to New Jersey. The immature forms of the heartworms (microfilaria) are spread from dog to dog by mosquitoes. The adult heartworms live in the heart and in the pulmonary artery, causing damage which can lead to congestive heart failure. Many dogs with heartworms do not show signs of disease until they are exercised, when it is noticed that the dog does not have as much tolerance for exercise as it should. Treatment of a dog with adult heartworms can be danger-

Fig. 7.7. An airborne dog enjoying agility. This is a graphic
example of why it is so vital to keep dogs heartworm-free.

ous because the dying worms travel to the lungs and can cause blood clots there.
Administration of heartworm preventive is essential for performance dogs that
live in or travel to endemic areas (Fig. 7.7).

CONDITIONS OF THE RESPIRATORY SYSTEM

Brachycephalic Airway Obstruction Syndrome

Although their faces can be appealing, brachycephalic dogs are susceptible to a variety of physical problems associated with the shape of their heads.
During the process of genetically selecting for shorter faces, the bones of the
muzzle have become shortened. However, the skin of the muzzle and the tissues
of the mouth and throat did not shorten correspondingly. These tissues may be
folded over or bunched up, impeding airflow and making breathing difficult,
especially when the animal is stressed or exercised in warm weather.
Brachycephalic dogs may also have narrowed or flattened nostrils (stenotic
nares) which impair breathing. Other associated defects include elongation of
the soft palate (which can cover the opening of the trachea and impede airflow)
and distortion or collapse of the larynx, the uppermost part of the trachea. These
dogs may also suffer damage to the cornea because of protruding eyes or because
their eyelids may not cover the cornea completely. Some of these problems can
be corrected surgically, and it's not unheard of for some dogs to require several
thousand dollars worth of cosmetic surgery before they can adequately function.
Breeders of brachycephalic breeds have become much more aware of this re-

cently and some are trying to moderate the extremes of facial type sometimes seen in these breeds. Dogs that have such genetic problems surgically corrected may not be shown in conformation and should not be bred.

Kennel Cough

Dogs at performance events are exposed to many infectious agents. One of the most common is kennel cough, an upper respiratory condition caused by one or more highly infectious bacteria or viruses. These agents are readily transmitted from dog to dog in aerosols produced by coughing. Because many of the infectious agents survive a long time on clothing, toys, and other inanimate objects, it is important to keep your dog away from any dog that appears to have kennel cough. It is also very irresponsible for a person to bring a dog with kennel cough to a performance event. That single dog can infect dozens of others within a very short period of time.

Dogs with kennel cough have a dry, honking cough, often followed by retching. The cough is frequently worse after exercise. The incubation period of kennel cough (the period between becoming infected and showing signs of disease) is five to ten days. The clinical disease can last from a week to ten days unless the animal develops a secondary bacterial infection of the throat or lungs, in which case the condition can last for weeks. Persistent infections should be evaluated by a veterinarian. While most dogs will eventually clear themselves of the infectious agent, an occasional dog may become persistently infected and is capable of transmitting the infection to susceptible dogs for weeks or months. Although vaccines against kennel cough are available, vaccinated dogs can still get kennel cough because the vaccine does not protect against all of the many organisms that can cause the condition. Dogs with kennel cough should be kept at home and given only mild exercise until the signs have abated.

Fungal Pneumonia

A number of fungal organisms live in the soil, particularly in the Mississippi River valley and in the Southwest. These organisms can cause severe pneumonia in dogs. Dogs that work outdoors, especially hunting dogs (Fig. 7.8) and terriers, may be exposed to these organisms by digging or sniffing dirt. If the dog's immune system is suppressed, either by age, stress, or corticosteroid administration, or if a large number of organisms are inhaled, the fungal organisms may replicate within the lungs and cause severe disease.

A dog with fungal pneumonia will have difficulty breathing and may have a cough. In addition, it will probably show signs of systemic illness, such as a low-grade fever, reduced appetite, and malaise. A diagnosis can only be

Fig. 7.8. Hunting dogs come into contact with many soil organisms.

made by a veterinarian after performing a clinical examination, taking blood for a complete blood count and biochemical profile, taking pulmonary radiographs, and studying material aspirated from the lung. In some cases, a biopsy may be necessary for a definitive diagnosis. It is very important that the veterinarian persist in identifying the cause of the pneumonia because, if left untreated, fungal pneumonia can be fatal. It is also critical that the veterinarian not treat the animal with corticosteroids, as this can cause immunosuppression and permit the organisms to spread from a local site throughout the body.

Treatment for fungal pneumonia involves long-term administration of antifungal agents. These drugs can be toxic, particularly to the kidneys, and animals being treated must be monitored for signs of toxicity.

CONDITIONS OF THE GASTROINTESTINAL TRACT

Pancreatitis

The pancreas secretes enzymes that digest proteins, fats, and carbohydrates. Even slight damage to the pancreas may be enough to cause these enzymes to spill out of the cells where they are stored, causing damage to the pancreas itself and to surrounding tissues (pancreatitis). There are many causes of pancreatitis, and it can be difficult to determine the specific cause in any given dog. Pancreatitis is associated with overfeeding (particularly in over-weight dogs), changes in diet, or excessive fat in the diet. A number of drugs can contribute to pancreatitis, including diuretics, antibiotics, and steroids. Systemic viral diseases can also cause pancreatitis. Pancreatitis can result from abdominal trauma in which the pancreas is damaged and leaks its enzymes. Hereditary factors may also be important in pancreatitis, since the condition is seen more frequently in certain breeds and lines within breeds.

A dog with pancreatitis will be depressed, will not want to eat, and may vomit and/or have diarrhea. These signs may be mild and gradual in onset, coming and going over a period of weeks, or they may be immediate and severe, leading to acute collapse. Treatment includes fasting, treatment of the gastrointestinal upset, rest, and intravenous fluids if necessary. A dog that has suffered a bout of pancreatitis should be maintained on a low fat diet. It will always be susceptible to recurrent bouts of pancreatitis but usually can lead an active life as a performance dog.

Canine Parvovirus

Canine parvovirus enteritis was first identified as a new disease in 1978. Because it was a new disease, dogs did not have immunity, and the virus swept through dog populations throughout the world, killing thousands. An effective vaccine was developed and put into use within three years, quickly reducing the number of deaths.

Parvovirus can stay viable in the environment for long periods of time, and it is not killed by many commercially available disinfectants. One of the best disinfecting agents to use against parvovirus is liquid chlorine bleach.

The hallmark of parvovirus infection is bloody diarrhea. Mildly affected dogs may recover in one or two days, but severely affected dogs become depressed and dehydrated and may die in a matter of days. Treatment involves supportive care including rest, dietary management, and intravenous fluids to counteract dehydration. The severity of the disease is dependent on the degree of immunity that the dog has to the virus. Animals with inadequate immunity, especially puppies, still continue to die of parvovirus enteritis despite treatment. Certain breeds, such as Doberman Pinschers and Rottweilers, seem to be more susceptible to severe parvoviral diarrhea.

Fig. 7.9. Large dogs with deep chests are more likely to suffer from gastric torsion.

Gastric Torsion

Gastric dilation and torsion (bloat) is a serious medical emergency with a high rate of mortality. In this condition, the dog's stomach becomes dilated with gas and may twist upon itself, blocking off blood flow to the stomach and preventing gastric emptying. This results in further buildup of gas, and initiates a vicious cycle. The actual cause of the condition is not known, but a recent study at Purdue University revealed several factors that predispose dogs to gastric torsion. Large dogs with deep, narrow chests, such as Doberman Pinschers, Irish Wolfhounds, and Borzoi have a higher incidence of gastric torsion than smaller dogs (Fig. 7.9). Another predisposing factor is eating rapidly. Dogs that are picky, slow eaters seem to have a lower incidence of bloat. Interestingly, the researchers found an association between stress and bloat. Dogs that bloat are more likely to have experienced a stressful event in the previous few hours. An unexpected finding of the study was that dogs that exercised before or after eating did not have an increased incidence of bloat.

Gastric torsion is one of the most important medical emergencies in the dog. A dog with gastric torsion will have a distended abdomen and will retch, salivate, and have trouble breathing. It may pace back and forth and appear very uncomfortable. If the dog is not given veterinary treatment within a few hours of developing gastric torsion, it will most likely die. The veterinarian will insert a stomach tube to try to remove the gas and may perform surgery to prevent the stomach from twisting again. Even after the stomach is decompressed, there is still the risk of death for several days afterward, because the stomach releases toxic substances that cause cardiac arrhythmias. Because it is such an acute, life-threatening condition, a dog that develops gastric torsion when alone is usually found dead by its owner. Dogs that have suffered from gastric torsion should be fed multiple small feedings each day rather than a single large meal.

GENERAL SYSTEMIC CONDITIONS

Ehrlichiosis and Rocky Mountain Spotted Fever

These two infectious diseases are transmitted by ticks and cause similar clinical syndromes in the dog. Canine ehrlichiosis is caused by a poorly understood infectious organism called *Ehrlichia canis* which inhabits the dog's white blood cells. Rocky Mountain spotted fever is caused by an organism called *Rickettsia rickettsiae* which lives in the cells lining blood vessels. Both organisms cause a wide range of clinical signs, including fever, loss of appetite, swollen lymph nodes, difficulty breathing, and hemorrhages on the skin and mucous membranes. Unless they receive appropriate antibiotic treatment, affected dogs can die. Therefore, a prompt, accurate diagnosis is essential. If your dog becomes ill after a tick bite, he should be tested for antibodies to these organisms and treated with tetracycline or doxycycline for at least four weeks to ensure elimination of the organism. Always remove ticks from your dog carefully, by gently pulling until they let go. Never squash a tick between your fingers, because Rocky Mountain spotted fever can be transmitted to humans.

Epilepsy

Epilepsy is a condition in which a dog periodically experiences seizures. A seizure is a disturbance of brain activity that usually appears as uncontrolled muscular activity. Seizures may be caused by an injury, such as a blow to the head, but frequently there is no identifiable cause.

Seizures can occur at any time, or they may be triggered by excitement, fatigue, bright lights, estrus, or changes in a dog's routine. Dogs are generally apprehensive or disoriented prior to a seizure and may have bizarre behavior, such as snapping at the air. During the seizure, the dog may lose consciousness and may have uncontrolled muscle movements, such as paddling or head shaking. Urination, defecation, and salivation may also occur. After the seizure, the dog may be either overexcited or depressed and may be weak and uncoordinated. This can last from a few minutes to several days. Occasionally, the seizure does not stop on its own, a condition known as status epilepticus. A dog in this condition must get veterinary attention immediately. Although some dogs may have one or only a few seizures in a lifetime, unfortunately, in many, the frequency and severity of seizures increases over the lifetime of the animal.

A history and description of the seizures is very important to make a diagnosis of idiopathic (unknown cause) epilepsy. The diagnosis is made if no brain lesion or other cause for the seizures can be found following a complete neurological workup. Unfortunately, a diagnosis of epilepsy is frequently made after a dog is several years old and, tragically, has already been bred. A classical example was a Border Collie bitch owned by a friend of mine. Brigitte had great potential for sheep herding. At the age of four years, she was bred to one of the top herding dogs in the United States. Shortly after whelping a litter of seven puppies, she had her first seizure, and more seizures soon followed. She was placed on phenobarbital but required very high doses just to reduce the frequency of seizures. The drug made her very drowsy. Three of her puppies developed epilepsy before they were a year old, and by the age of three years, all had had seizures. The seizures were so severe in several of the pups that they had to be euthanized. By the time her puppies were one and a half years of age, Brigitte's seizures became uncontrollable and she, too, had to be put to sleep. The owner of the stud dog claimed that his dog had never had seizures and that there was no history of epilepsy in his ancestors, the implication being that the condition was passed only by the dam. Unfortunately, this story is not an unusual one. It illustrates how frustrating and disappointing epilepsy can be.

Because of side effects, treatment for seizures in performance dogs should only be instituted if seizures are occurring more often than once every six weeks. There are currently only a few medications that are effective in treating epilepsy in dogs, and they all have side-effects such as depression and a reduction in the dog's energy level. This can impede the career of a performance dog. The medications do not cure epilepsy, and in most cases must be continued for the life of the animal. Veterinarians consider seizure control to be defined as a 50 percent reduction in seizure frequency without drug intoxication. It is estimated that seizure control is achieved with phenobarbital in about 60 percent of affected dogs.

Most physicians agree that people with epilepsy can and should participate in sports once their condition has been stabilized by drugs. It can be presumed that the same principles hold true for dogs with epilepsy. There are no published reports of a person having a seizure during an athletic event. I have, however, observed a dog suffering a seizure during an obedience trial and another dog having a seizure right after an agility trial. At least one of these dogs was on anticonvulsant medication. Dogs with epilepsy can participate in performance events but should be watched carefully, especially if they have had a seizure at an event. Special care should be taken when a dog with epilepsy swims, because if a seizure occurs while the dog is swimming, it may drown.

Hypothyroidism

Hypothyroidism is a syndrome in which there is a deficiency in the amount of thyroid hormone being produced by the thyroid gland. The thyroid gland may be attacked and permanently damaged by the body (an autoimmune reaction), or it may just cease to produce sufficient hormone for unknown reasons. Hypothyroidism occurs in many breeds of dogs, but the incidence is particularly high in Doberman Pinschers, Golden Retrievers, Irish Setters, Shetland Sheepdogs, and several other breeds.

Hypothyroidism generally develops in middle-aged dogs (usually over 4 years of age). There are many different signs of hypothyroidism, and some can be quite subtle. Probably the most obvious signs are hair loss, excessive shedding, or a dry coat. Dogs with severe, undiagnosed hypothyroidism may be almost completely bald. Other signs include mental dullness and lethargy, weight gain, sterility, failure of females to come into heat, and intolerance to cold (Fig. 7.10). A definitive diagnosis can only be made on the basis of blood tests to determine the baseline levels of circulating thyroid hormones in the blood. Because of the wide variety of clinical manifestations of this disease and the variability of blood test methods and results, a veterinary task force met in August, 1996 and outlined the specific criteria needed to make a diagnosis of

Fig. 7.10. Labrador Retriever returning from a water retrieve. Hypothyroidism can affect a dog's tolerance to cold.

hypothyroidism. Diagnosis is made by examining the combined results of a clinical examination, complete blood counts, blood chemistry, and urinalysis.

Treatment of hypothyroidism involves lifetime supplementation with thyroid hormones. Dogs that are supplemented usually do quite well, but supplementation does cause the remaining thyroid tissue to cease functioning. This can have serious effects if the therapy is discontinued after long-term treatment because the thyroid gland will not recover for months, if ever.

Von Willebrand's Disease

Von Willebrand's Disease (VWD) is a type of bleeding disorder or hemophilia. Normal blood contains many proteins that help it to clot when a blood vessel is damaged or cut. Dogs with von Willebrand's disease have reduced levels of one of these clotting proteins, called von Willebrand's factor, so that their blood does not clot adequately.

VWD is caused by a mutation of an autosomal gene. The gene has incomplete dominance so that dogs differ in their expression of the disease. There are over 50 breeds of dogs in which VWD has been reported, and it can also occur in mixed breeds. One report suggested that at least 72 percent of Doberman Pinschers carry the gene. Other breeds with a high incidence include the Pembroke Welsh Corgi, the Shetland Sheepdog, Standard and Miniature Poodles, and the Scottish Terrier.

Dogs with VWD bleed easily from a variety of places, including the nose and gums, and may have blood in their urine and stools periodically. They also bleed profusely when cut, either by accident or during surgical procedures. The problem may first be noticed when the owner accidentally cuts the quick of the nails and the nail continues to bleed for 30 minutes or more. An affected animal that has never had any noticeable bleeding episodes may be first diagnosed when life-threatening bleeding occurs following minor surgery such as neutering. In severe cases, VWD might prevent a dog from being able to undergo elective surgical procedures such as teeth cleaning, castration, or spaying. Severely affected dogs can die after being cut by accident.

The severity of the condition is dependent on how much von Willebrand factor the dog produces. The normal range for von Willebrand factor is greater than 60 percent. Dogs with levels of 40 to 60 percent are considered carriers and those with less than 40 percent are considered affected. Dogs with levels in the 40 to 60 percent range should be used in a breeding program cautiously (to a mate testing well within the normal range), if at all. Dogs with levels in the abnormal range may be bleeders and are at risk for transmitting the VWD gene to their offspring. They should not be bred. The incidence of VWD is increasing in the dog population, suggesting that affected dogs continue to be bred.

The level of von Willebrand factor may be altered temporarily in bitches in heat, during pregnancy, or during lactation. It may also be affected in dogs that are ill, have thyroid disease, or have been vaccinated within 14 days. It is essential that the blood sample for a VWD test be taken correctly and shipped to a laboratory under strictly controlled conditions.

Hypothyroidism can increase the bleeding tendency of a dog with VWD. Any dog with a low level of von Willebrand's factor should also be tested for hypothyroidism, and treated with thyroid hormone if necessary. Bleeding may also be increased by physical, and psychological stress, and by concurrent infectious diseases. There is no treatment for VWD, and affected animals must be prevented from having surgery if at all possible. Desmopressin (DDAVP) may be used to temporarily increase the level of von Willebrand factor to permit an affected dog to have necessary surgery. Depending on the severity of bleeding, an affected dog's activities may have to be curtailed, possibly for life. Animals with von Willebrand's disease always risk lameness due to mild trauma and bleeding into the joints. Supplementation with thyroid hormone may control bleeding in animals with mild to moderate VWD and low thyroid hormone levels.

Fig. 7.11. The Border Collie is an example of a breed that loves to work, often regardless of the temperature.

Hyperthermia (Heatstroke)

The dog's body produces heat by muscular exercise, by eating, and by a variety of metabolic processes. The ideal air temperature for a sedentary dog is 75°F (24°C) with low humidity. At this temperature, the dog's body neither gains nor loses heat, so the dog does not have to expend any energy to maintain its body temperature. However, even this moderate temperature is too warm for an active dog.

Muscular activity can significantly increase a dog's body temperature. The body temperature of a dog undertaking intense muscular effort, such as flyball competition, may temporarily rise to as high as 106°F (42°C). As the air temperature approaches or surpasses the body temperature, the body is unable to give off heat and begins to store it, adding to the heat created by muscular effort.

The dog is burdened by having limited mechanisms for coping with overheating. Panting is the main mechanism used by dogs to dissipate internal heat. The tongue is able to expand to approximately twice its normal size, increasing the surface area for heat exchange. Blood vessels in the tongue dilate to bring more blood up to the surface of the tongue to be cooled. Heat is also dissipated through the mucous membranes on the inside of the mouth and through contact of the cooler air with the lungs. In addition, dogs perspire on the pads of their feet. Walk your dog over a shiny floor on a warm day and you can see the imprint of each foot as he leaves a sweaty paw print on the smooth surface. Many obedience dogs leave a record of where their feet have been on the mats in the obedience rings. Humidity inhibits the evaporation of moisture on the tongue, mouth, and pads, and thus can contribute to the development of heatstroke. Dogs may also try to lower their body temperature by seeking cool places, by not eating (therefore producing less internal heat), and by reducing their activity level.

Hyperthermia can be induced in performance dogs by extreme exercise on a day with moderately warm temperatures (especially with high humidity) or even by moderate exercise on a very hot day. In either case, a dog's cooling mechanisms may be overwhelmed. It is essential that you be sensitive to the possibility of your dog becoming overheated. Always remember that our own mechanisms for coping with heat are far superior to those of our dogs. Therefore, if you are uncomfortable, your dog must be very uncomfortable. Performance dogs have two further strikes against them. They have been trained by us to perform, and many will do so despite extreme physical discomfort (Fig. 7.11). In addition, they are not able to communicate to us verbally and thus cannot tell us how warm they feel. Dogs must have access to drinking water at all times in hot weather, especially when being trained or shown. In the summer, clubs hosting performance events should provide pools with cool water so that dogs can be immersed to cool down, if necessary.

Puppies are particularly susceptible to heatstroke. At a recent dog show I attended on a summer day with temperatures in the low eighties and humidity of about 70 percent, an announcer called for any veterinarian on the grounds to go to Ring 11 immediately. There, a three month-old Pembroke Welsh Corgi puppy lay suffering from heatstroke. The puppy had been kept in the shade under a tent and had not been exercising, but was still critically ill. This illustrates how important it is to always be conscious of the possibility of heatstroke in dogs.

Just as with people, individual dogs differ in their ability to control overheating. In people, gradual acclimatization to hot weather over a period of two weeks significantly reduces the risk of hyperthermia. Two black Labrador Retrievers, an 11-year-old Field Trial Champion named Waffle and a three-year-old obedience dog named Albert, demonstrated these differences. Both Waffle and Albert were competing in obedience trials together during a warm spell in April. It was obvious that Albert found the heat just unbearable, while Waffle was totally unconcerned. Perhaps this difference in response was just a matter of individual sensitivities to the heat, or perhaps it was because Waffle, the Field

Trial Champion, was conditioned to perform in all kinds of weather, whereas Albert had only been trained in obedience during moderate weather conditions.

The signs of heat stroke include rapid, noisy breathing, a red, enlarged tongue, thick saliva, body temperature above 106°F, staggering, and weakness. The treatment of hyperthermia involves immediately cooling the dog's body surface with alcohol and/or cool water. The dog should be wrapped in towels soaked in cold water and transported to a veterinarian as soon as possible. There it will receive further treatment, including intravenous fluids and perhaps cool water enemas as well as treatment for shock, if necessary. If a dog with heat-stroke remains untreated, it may suffer fatal pulmonary edema and brain damage.

Hypothermia

Small dogs, puppies, and dogs with short coats are particularly suscep-tible to hypothermia (Fig. 7.12). Dogs participating in winter performance events and sports such as sledding and cross-country skiing can also suffer from hypothermia. In addition, hypothermia may be a concern in field trial dogs which have to swim long distances in cool fall weather. When a dog gets wet, the coat loses much of its insulating property. To prevent hypothermia, dogs should be dried off as soon as possible after swimming in cool weather and after working or playing in the snow.

Dogs suffering from hypothermia will appear tired and will shiver violently. They will have pale, clammy gums, and will be lethargic and con-fused. After a period of time, if untreated, the shivering will stop, and the dog will become listless. This is followed by coma and death.

The main principle in the treatment of hypothermia is to warm the dog as rapidly as possible. This can be accomplished by wrapping it in a blanket or coat, or, if the dog is already wet, by placing it in a warm bath or by laying warm water packs on the chest and stomach. The dog should then be rubbed dry vigorously with towels or warmed with an electric hair dryer. When the dog starts to move about, it should be given a little high energy food such as honey.

Dogs can suffer from frostbite, especially of the ears, tail, and scrotum. Owners of dogs that participate in winter sports such as skijoring, should always be aware of the possibility of frostbite. Most commonly, animals that are af-fected are those which are not used to spending time out in the cold and which have been exposed to subzero temperatures for several hours. The affected skin will be very pale and cold to the touch. After thawing, the skin will be red and

Fig. 7.12. Puppies are especially susceptible to hypothermia — their periods outside should be brief and full of activity.

may peel. If the frostbite is severe enough, the skin may die and scar tissue will form. If frostbite is suspected, the skin should be handled very gently and should be thawed by applying warm (not hot) water.

Snake Bite

Hunting dogs, field trial dogs, and herding dogs suffer more often than other breeds from snake bites because they are frequently outdoors running in open country. There are three factors that are important in determining how serious a snake bite is: the size of the dog, the kind of snake, and the location of the bite. Bites of venomous snakes are more serious in smaller dogs because the snake secretes the same amount of toxin regardless of the size of its target. Thus, a smaller dog will have a higher concentration of the venom in its body than a larger dog.

Snakes secrete two classes of venoms. Most of the venomous snakes in North America, including rattlesnakes, water moccasins, and copperheads, secrete toxins that cause the red blood cells to break down and the blood to clot, resulting in local tissue damage. Dogs bitten by these kinds of snakes develop a large area of swelling at the location of the bite. The place where the fangs punctured the skin may be seen in the area of greatest swelling. The clinical signs will depend on the location of the bite. If the dog is bitten in the leg, it may be lame. If it is bitten in the face it may have trouble breathing due to swelling of tissues of the muzzle.

Fig. 7.13. Dogs can get "cold tail" after swimming or being bathed in cold water.

The other kind of venom damages the nerves, causing paralysis. The only snake native to North America that secretes this kind of toxin is the coral snake. Dogs that are bitten by this kind of snake generally do not have much swelling at the area of the bite. They become disoriented, have difficulty breathing and swallowing, and may have convulsions. They then develop paralysis, which may become so severe that it causes respiratory failure and death.

If your dog has been bitten by a snake, do not waste valuable time applying ice, cutting into the bitten area, or applying a tourniquet. Instead, keep the dog quiet and transport it to a veterinarian as soon as possible. The veterinarian will administer an antivenin (antidote for snake venom) and provide supportive treatment such as intravenous fluids, anti-inflammatory drugs, and antibiotics. Dogs bitten by the coral snake need immediate intensive care.

There are many other venomous animals that can cause anything from local swelling to widespread systemic effects in dogs. Some of these include spiders (black widow, brown recluse), hymenoptera (bees, wasps, hornets, etc.), caterpillars, centipedes, lizards, toads, and scorpions. Hymenoptera stings can be very serious, particularly if there are many stings or if an animal develops a hypersensitivity reaction to the sting. In humans, 50 hornet stings can be fatal, and a single sting can be fatal in a person who has a severe hypersensitivity reaction. Hymenoptera stings should be treated by removing the stinger if necessary (only bees leave the stinger in) and applying ice packs to decrease the swelling. If the swelling continues, or if the dog shows signs of systemic illness, it should be taken to a veterinarian.

Cold Tail

This is a disorder of unknown cause, mainly seen in Sporting and Working breeds, in which a dog's tail becomes paralyzed for a period of several days. The condition is never discussed in veterinary texts, yet it is well-known among breeders and handlers. It is called "cold tail" because it often occurs after a dog has been swimming in cold water or after it has been washed with cold water, such as with a garden hose (Fig. 7.13). However, it can also occur without such a history. The dog develops a temporary, partial, or total paralysis of the tail. It may first be noticed because the dog is holding its tail down or not wagging it. Sometimes the dog may turn and look at its tail as if it cannot identify the appendage that is attached to its back end! Some dogs may bite at the tail as if it itches or prickles. Generally the tail regains its ability to move in one to three days. Very occasionally a dog will have repeated episodes of cold tail and may even develop a permanently sensitive tail.

Reading List

Delbert G. Carlson D.V.M., James M. Griffin MD. *Dog Owners Home Veterinary Handbook*. Howell Book House, NY, 1980

Michelle Bamberger D.V.M. *Help! The Quick Guide to First Aid for Your Dog*. Howell Book House, New York, 1993.

Could a performance dog function as well with medication as without? The question involves ethics as well as the dog's safety and health.

8.

MEDICATIONS

AND PERFORMANCE

*The dog has seldom been successful in
pulling man up to its level of sagacity,
but man has frequently dragged the dog
down to his.*

James Thurber

THE BASICS OF PHARMACOLOGY

For a drug to have an effect, it must enter the body and be delivered to the site at which it will act. Drugs can be taken into the body by many different means. They can be ingested orally and then absorbed into the body through the lining of the stomach or the small intestine. They can be injected under the skin, where they diffuse slowly into the blood stream, or intramuscularly, where they are more quickly taken up by blood vessels. Drugs can also be injected directly into a blood vessel (usually a vein) or directly into the target tissue (for example, a joint). Some drugs can be absorbed directly through the skin. Carrier agents such as dimethylsulfoxide (DMSO) can also be used to carry a drug rapidly across the skin and into the blood stream.

As a general rule, drugs given orally are slower to reach effective levels within the blood stream because they must first dissolve before being absorbed. However, effective levels are maintained in the blood for a long time after oral administration. At the other end of the spectrum, drugs that are administered intravenously reach effective levels immediately, but the levels are not maintained as long because the drug is rapidly removed from the blood by the liver and kidneys. Subcutaneous and intramuscular administration have intermediate absorption and clearance times.

Once in the body, the drug is delivered by the blood stream to the site at which it will act. The location of action is determined by small molecules on the surfaces of cells called receptors. The drug attaches to the receptors and is drawn into the cell. Receptors are generally very specific — they will only permit certain drugs into the cell. If there are receptors for a certain drug in many tissues in the body, then that drug will have widespread effects throughout the body. On the other hand, if there are receptors for a certain drug in only one location in the body, then that drug will have a localized effect in that organ only. For example, insulin acts on virtually every cell in the body, whereas a tranquilizer acts predominantly on cells in the brain.

Side effects occur when a drug has effects on tissues other than the target tissue. For example, antihistamines are commonly used by people suffering from allergies to decrease nasal secretions. However, cells in the brain also have receptors for antihistamines, and their effect on the brain is to cause drowsiness. Side effects are somewhat like weeds in a garden. They are doing the right thing but in the wrong place. Because the percentage of cells that have receptors for a drug is usually small, only a small fraction of most drugs actually reaches cells with receptors and has an effect. The rest of the drug is eventually eliminated.

Individual animals vary in their absorption and utilization of drugs, so drug dosages should always be considered on an individual basis. The amount of a drug recommended for one animal should never be used on another animal without first consulting a veterinarian.

Once inside the cell, the drug has a biochemical effect on cellular processes. The drug may have a direct effect, such as blocking the ability of nerves to feel pain, or it may set in motion a series of biochemical events that ultimately produce the desired effects.

Once a drug has had its effect, it does not remain in its active form but is changed to an inactive form so that it can be excreted by the body. There are two major organs that are involved in the elimination of drugs: the liver and the kidneys. The liver is responsible for changing, or detoxifying, many drugs. Liver cells contain enzymes which metabolize many different biochemical substances, producing nontoxic metabolites that are then excreted in the urine. Excretion of these metabolites by the kidneys is the reason that samples of urine are taken for drug testing.

ADVERSE DRUG REACTIONS

The suggested doses for drugs are just that — suggested doses. These doses have been arrived at by testing a wide variety of dogs of different sizes and breeds. However, they are not always right for every dog. Just as in humans, dogs have individual resistances and sensitivities to drugs. There are many reasons why a drug may have a different effect in one animal than another (Table 8.1). Doses for drugs are usually given in relationship to body weight. A very obese dog, however, may weigh twice what its normal body weight should be, but the extra weight consists almost entirely of fat. If the drug is not soluble in fat, the nonfat portion of that dog's body may be exposed to twice the amount of drug because the drug was administered on the basis of body weight alone. If, on the other hand, the drug is absorbed by fat, it may be difficult to achieve and maintain effective levels of the drug in an obese dog because the excess fat absorbs the drug. Some breeds have an increased likelihood of hypersensitivity reactions to certain drugs. Sighthounds (in particular, Salukis, Greyhounds and Borzoi) and some Border Collies are sensitive to a number of anesthetic agents (Fig. 8.1).

The incidence of adverse drug reactions is much greater in very young and in very old dogs. The tissues of dogs less than 30 days old may not have all of the biochemical components needed to metabolize a drug. Older dogs may have developed a hypersensitivity to a drug or may have organ dysfunction, such as liver failure, which can reduce the amount of drug metabolized by the body and increase the likelihood of toxic effects. Pregnant animals may be more sensitive to some drugs because alterations in body weight and circulation may affect tissue distribution of the drug. Animals with inhalant allergies seem to be more susceptible to adverse drug reactions.

Table 8.1
Reasons for
Adverse Drug Reactions

Obesity
Individual susceptibility
Breed susceptibility
Liver dysfunction
Kidney dysfunction
Age
Pregnancy
Drug interactions

Fig. 8.1. Borzoi, Salukis, and Greyhounds can be sensitive to a number of anesthetic agents.

Finally, drug interactions can increase or decrease the effects of a drug in a given tissue. For example, a number of drugs, including glucocorticoids, anticonvulsants, aspirin, and phenylbutazone, can alter the level of administered thyroid hormone in the body. The incidence of adverse drug reactions increases exponentially when more than one drug is administered because of the potential for drug interactions.

Adverse drug reactions may be manifested in dogs in a number of ways. One type of adverse drug reaction occurs when the dose of the drug is too high or alterations in availability expose the tissues to abnormally high levels, causing toxic effects. The signs of this type of drug reaction vary according to the particular drug involved. One of the most life threatening reactions is anaphylaxis. This is an acute systemic allergic reaction, that can lead to shock. A dog experiencing anaphylaxis has cardiovascular collapse: the heart rhythm may become irregular, and the blood pressure lowers suddenly. The dog may begin to pace and may pant heavily, and it may vomit and/or have diarrhea. It is essential that dogs experiencing anaphylaxis or an adverse drug reaction are provided with veterinary care immediately. The veterinarian will provide life support, enhance elimination of the drug, and if possible, administer an antidote or antagonist.

SIDE EFFECTS/TOXICITY OF SOME DRUGS

Because drugs circulate throughout the body, they may have effects other than those for which they were administered. Many of the antibacterial or antifungal agents can have toxic side effects. For example, tetracyclines can discolor puppies' teeth and slow bone development. For these reasons, their use is not recommended either in pregnant dogs or puppies. Gentamicin, a broad-spectrum antibiotic, can cause kidney damage; dogs taking this antibiotic longterm should be monitored for signs of early renal damage. If this occurs, the drug can be discontinued and the kidney given time to repair itself. Glucocorticoids cause increased drinking and urination and can increase the frequency and/or severity of seizures in dogs with epilepsy. There are many drugs that act on the brain, causing drowsiness, weakness, and lethargy. Some are listed in Table 8.2. A number of medications can impair the scenting ability of dogs. Some of these include dimethylsulfoxide (DMSO), codeine and morphine (used in cough suppressants), amphetamines, and glucocorticoids. Because the administration of glucocorticoids can affect the scenting ability of some dogs, their use is avoided in drug and bomb detection dogs. Latent epilepsy (in an animal which has not yet had a seizure) may be unmasked during corticosteroid use. Animals that have von Willebrand's Disease may be more prone to bleeding episodes when treated with nonsteroidal anti-inflammatory drugs such as aspirin.

It is essential that you ask your veterinarian about possible side effects whenever she prescribes medications for your dog. The veterinarian may not be familiar with the athletic exercises your dog must perform and therefore may not realize that a side effect that may go unnoticed in a house pet can be a significant impediment in a performance dog. For example, veterinarians sometimes prescribe phenobarbital for a dog that has had a single seizure. The weakness and lethargy caused by this drug can impair a dog's athletic performance. Therefore, it is prudent to first determine whether the dog will have more seizures and, if so, at what frequency, before instituting treatment with this drug. A note should be made in the dog's health records of the possible side effects of prescribed drugs and the dog observed carefully for them.

DRUGS, PERFORMANCE, AND ETHICS

The dictionary defines ethics as "the moral principle by which a person is guided." When applied to sports, this ideal would state that the athlete, and in

Table 8.2
Drugs That Can
Cause Weakness or Lethargy

Antidiarrheals with sedatives

Anticonvulsant medication

Antihistamines

Tranquilizers

Some antibiotics

Diuretic agents

Vasodilators

the case of canine performance events, the coach/handler strives to succeed in the sport by his/her own unaided effort and does not seek an unfair advantage.

There are two major factors in the attainment of success in athletic events, whether human or canine. First, the competitor must be capable of superior athletic ability. Secondly, the competitor must be trained and handled by a coach with forethought and knowledge. In both human sports and canine sports, people have tried to improve upon these two basic components by providing ergogenic (*ergon* = work; *gennan* = to produce) aids to enhance performance.

The issue of performance-enhancing drugs has been investigated much more thoroughly in human athletics, where drugs and other ergogenic aids have been used for centuries. At the level of Olympic competition, where the stakes are highest, organizers have had to grapple with which drugs will be banned and which are acceptable for the athlete to use. The principles that guide their decisions are that the athlete should be allowed to take drugs which permit him or her to be healthy enough to train and compete (to cure, control, or comfort). However, the athlete should not be permitted to take drugs that may artificially enhance performance or increase the excretion of performance-enhancing drugs, thereby reducing the likelihood of detection. With this in mind, the International Olympic Committee has a long list of drugs that are banned. These can be broadly classified into the following groups: 1) stimulants (such as amphetamines and caffeine), sympathomimetic drugs (those that mimic the effects of the sympathetic nervous system), and narcotics (such as codeine and cocaine); 2) depressants and tranquilizers; 3) anabolic steroids; 4) diuretics, which may be taken in an effort to increase the excretion of illegal drugs in the urine.

The use of performance-enhancing drugs has not been formally addressed to any extent by the bodies that govern canine performance events, except for the organizers of Greyhound races. The widespread use of performance-enhancing (or perceived performance-enhancing) drugs in dogs suggests that the issue should be addressed. When questioned regarding their policy on performance-enhancing drugs, the American Kennel Club refers to their rule that a dog should not have its appearance altered by artificial means. The broader interpretation of this rule is that a dog in competition should not receive performance-enhancing drugs since they would alter its appearance in performance events (Fig. 8.2). On this basis, one could unequivocally state that a dog that has been given anabolic steroids should not be allowed to compete, nor should a dog that has been given amphetamines or caffeine to increase its energy level.

However, on considering this issue further, it becomes less clear cut. For example, may an old, slightly arthritic dog be given aspirin to relieve pain when it is competing in a Veterans class? The strictest interpretation would argue that he should not. Should a dog scheduled to be shown in conformation on Saturday that develops a small, localized skin infection on the stomach after being cut by brambles be given antibiotics to treat the infection? The strictest interpretation of the current guidelines suggests that the dog should not be given the antibiotic, or if it is, it should not compete. The absolute strictest interpretation would be that a dog that has been diagnosed as hypothyroid, and which will have to be treated with thyroid hormone for the rest of its life, should not compete again. Nor should a bitch compete that has been given Ovaban® or Cheque® to delay its heat cycle. Nor should any dog on medication to prevent seizures compete. Yet we know that they do.

I would propose that canine athletic events use the same guidelines as the Olympics. This would mean that it would be permissible and ethical to administer drugs that cure, control, or comfort, but any drug that would give a dog an unfair advantage in performance would not be permitted (Fig. 8.3).

With the exception of diuretics, all classes of ergogenic drugs that are used in human athletes are being used in performance dogs. To that list might be added the following: 1) drugs such as atropine and thyroid hormone that improve (or are believed to improve) physical appearance, and 2) drugs to control heat cycles in the bitch and that have secondary effects on behavior (Table 8.3).

Stimulants are used to enhance a dog's performance in athletic competition or to make a dog appear more active and bright. Their use is not uncommon in the conformation ring and is unconsciously promoted by judges who reward dogs with a very showy attitude, even in breeds for which this is not natural. A competitor who has a dog with a more businesslike temperament may feel that a stimulant such as caffeine will make the dog look brighter and prevent it from getting tired as quickly, especially if it goes on to Group and Best-in-Show competition. Many competitors believe that guidelines by the American Kennel Club on the performance of obedience dogs stating that a dog must demonstrate the "utmost in willingness and enjoyment" (Fig. 8.4) have led to further use of stimulants in obedience dogs.

The use of stimulants is not without consequences. Studies of people taking stimulants to enhance performance have shown that these drugs significantly increase the risk of hyperthermia (heat stroke) and, in large doses, may lead to disorientation, nervousness, and anxiety. Amphetamines and cocaine are addictive and can be fatal in people. Occasionally, cocaine is administered to dogs as a central nervous system stimulant. Dogs that have been treated with cocaine have increased muscular tone, a rapid heart rate, irregular heart rhythms, and an increased respiratory rate. If overdosed, the cardiovascular effects can be life-threatening, and there are no specific antidotes for cocaine intoxication.

Depressants are more commonly used in the conformation ring than in other performance events and may be used to tone down the nervousness of an animal, especially one that is not well socialized or that is hyperactive. There is probably little benefit to the use of tranquilizers in events such as obedience or agility, or others in which speed and precision are needed, unless a dog is very hyperactive. If overdosed, these drugs can cause depression of the respiratory and cardiovascular systems and even death.

Anabolic steroids were developed by scientists commissioned by Adolf Hitler, who wanted a drug to make the SS more aggressive. These drugs were also shown to have some effects in the healing of fractures and in the building up of muscle. The 1988 Olympics, in which the winner of the 100-meter race tested

Table 8.3 Classes of Performance-Enhancing Drugs Used in Dogs	
Class of Drug	*Examples*
Stimulants	Amphetamines, caffeine, cocaine
Depressants	Acepromazine, Valium®
Anabolic steroids	Winstrol-V®
Drugs to modify heat cycles	Ovaban®, Cheque®
Drugs to modify appearance	Atropine, thyroid hormone

Fig. 8.2. An Afghan Hound enjoying lure coursing. The AKC ruling is that dogs should not have their appearance altered by artificial means. This rule can be difficult to interpret.

Fig. 8.3. A Golden Retriever charges off to retrieve a downed bird. It is unethical to administer a drug that would give a dog an unfair advantage in competition.

Fig. 8.4. A Shetland Sheepdog demonstrating the "utmost in willingness and enjoyment."

positive for anabolic steroids, revealed just how widespread their use is even by
the most prominent athletes. In dogs, anabolic steroids are used in an effort to
produce a larger animal with more bone and coat, an advantage for some breeds
in conformation. These drugs are also used to improve dogs' muscular strength
in performance events requiring speed and strength. In humans, there is serious
doubt as to whether the anabolic steroids do actually increase growth. Although
anabolic steroids help to increase muscle mass if used with a program of heavy
weight training (particularly isotonic exercises, which, by the way, are difficult
to accomplish in dogs), they actually result in a decrease in stature if used in
young people because they cause premature closure of the growth plates of the
bones. These drugs also increase aggressiveness (unnecessary in any canine
sport!) and prolonged use can cause testicular atrophy and irreversible sterility.
In addition, they can cause enlargement of the prostate gland and can contribute
to prostatic cancer, heart disease, and liver damage.

Drugs to modify appearance have been used for years in dogs competing
in conformation shows. Many people who show breeds in which abundant coat
is rewarded administer thyroid hormone to their dogs, regardless of whether the
dog is producing sufficient thyroid hormone on its own. These people naively
think that the hormone merely grows coat when, in fact, its effects are much
broader. Hair growth is only a secondary effect, occurring only in dogs very
deficient in thyroid hormone. If given in excess, thyroid hormones will cause
tissue and muscle breakdown, as well as premature aging. Dogs overdosed with
thyroid hormone may become aggressive and hyperactive; they will drink and

urinate excessively and will be nervous. Once thyroid hormone is administered for several months, the thyroid gland will shut down its own production of thyroid hormone so that, if hormone administration is ceased, the thyroid is unable to compensate by producing its own.

Atropine is used in the eyes of dogs whose breed standards call for almond-shaped eyes. Atropine causes the pupils to dilate and the dog to squint. If a dog has rounded eyes, atropine can make them appear more almond-shaped. However, atropine can also be absorbed into the blood stream, causing dryness of the mouth, a decrease in blood pressure, and a slowing of the heart rate.

Drugs to modify heat cycles are used by competitors in obedience, field trials, hunting tests, and other competitions in which females in heat are prohibited from competing. Trainers and handlers have observed that these drugs sometimes alter a bitch's behavior (either depressing or increasing activity level) and have begun to use them with behavior alteration as a primary goal. These drugs, if used on a continuous basis, can cause permanent aberrations in the female's heat cycle, possibly leading to infertility.

Performance-modifying drugs are being administered to dogs in a variety of different performance events. But a little knowledge is a dangerous thing, and those administering these drugs are often not aware of the longterm problems they may be causing. I hope that a knowledge of some of the side effects of these drugs will give people cause to reconsider the value of their use. Unfortunately, to some people, winning is more important than the health of their dogs. Because the organizations that oversee canine performance events do not currently test for performance-enhancing drugs, ultimately the question of whether to administer performance-modifying drugs depends on an individual's ethics — the moral principles by which a person is guided.

Only when free of stress can a dog perform at his best.

9.

STRESS AND

THE PERFORMANCE DOG

Money will buy a pretty good dog,
but it won't buy the wag of its tail.
Josh Billings

Our understanding of stress and its effects on health and performance is only in its infancy in humans. Even less is understood about stress in dogs. One definition of stress is that it is a response (positive or negative) to environmental influences. Examples of things that cause stress in humans include major life events such as a death in the family, marriage, divorce, moving to a new house, and beginning a new job.

Wolves live in a well-defined physical and social environment. They have a territory which is marked out and guarded from encroachment by competitors. The wolves roam outside of this area to hunt but always return to the safety of these boundaries. In addition, each wolf knows where it stands within the hierarchy of the pack — which members of the pack are deemed superior and which are not.

The physical and social environment of a performance dog, however, is constantly changing. Our dogs travel by car or plane, visit new locations frequently, and some — especially those that are sent out with handlers — must cope with constant changes in their human and canine associates. After all of this, they are asked to stand proudly in the conformation ring, to tread water and concentrate on a handler giving hand signals 100 yards away across a pond, or to discriminate the scent of their owner from that of a steward who has been munching on potato chips! Is it any wonder they feel stressed? For a dog to cope with these changes and still perform at its peak, takes a flexibility and strength of temperament we often do not appreciate.

As trainers and handlers, we are frequently responsible for increasing the stress which our dogs experience during performance. Our own stress, expressed in body language such as tension, repetitive motions, and a change in the tone of the voice, is easily detected in dogs, who are experts in subtle body language. Our dogs, who are our companions during the other days of the week, are confused by the change in our behavior and this increases their own stress level.

Illness, no matter how mild, also creates stress in an animal. Chronic illness is particularly stressful in dogs and is the reason that dogs with degenerative joint disease may be irritable and may even bite humans who make friendly overtures.

PHYSIOLOGICAL EFFECTS OF STRESS
The body responds to stress both biochemically and neurologically, and these responses affect the immune system as well as the cardiovascular, respiratory, and gastrointestinal systems. One of the main physiological responses to stress is the release of endogenous (produced within the body) glucocorticoids. Because these steroids are produced by the body during stress, they are often referred to as stress hormones. (Glucocorticoids are not the same as anabolic steroids, which are used, without justification, as ergogenic aids.) Steroids affect virtually every cell in the body. They help the liver to produce more glucose, which is secreted into the blood to supply increased nutrients in the form of energy to the cells of the body. Steroids cause vasoconstriction, constricting the blood vessels of the skin. This permits the available blood to be redistributed to other areas, such as the brain and the muscles, where it may be needed more. Steroids increase the dog's appetite and induce an overall feeling of well-being. All of these functions can be important in the body's ability to respond to stress.

Steroids, however, can also lower the body's defenses against disease. An example of stress-induced disease in humans is cold sores. These annoying lesions are caused by a virus which, under normal conditions, lies dormant within the nerves supplying the face. If a person is stressed, endogenous steroids are released, lowering the body's defenses and allowing the virus to replicate and damage the skin of the lips. In dogs, stress can increase both susceptibility to infections and the severity of clinical disease due to infectious agents.

Stressful situations also induce a neurological response, orchestrated by the sympathetic arm of the autonomic nervous system. The sympathetic nerves, working in conjunction with adrenalin secreted from the adrenal glands, cause a variety of physiological changes in the body, including shifts in blood flow, changes in brain activity, and increased muscular strength.

At the molecular level, emotions are created by biochemical events within the brain. Whenever nerves transmit messages from one area of the brain to another, chemical substances, called neurotransmitters, are released. These substances can create the full range of psychological effects such as happiness, fear, tension, and many other emotions. The release of these biochemical messages is partly responsible for the feeling of stress. However, the study of the effects of these biochemical messengers is only in its infancy, and we have much to learn about how they work before we can devise means by which to modulate their effects.

PHYSICAL SIGNS OF STRESS

Humans frequently respond to stress by becoming tired. The same physiological responses occur in stressed dogs. However, a tired dog just doesn't look like it should in the conformation ring (Fig. 9.1). A tired dog cannot concentrate on its performance.

There are many abnormal behaviors that are thought to be at least partly a reflection of stress in dogs. These include self-mutilation, especially excessive licking and biting on the legs, sucking on the flank, repeated champing of the jaws, and tail chasing (in some dogs). Other unwanted behaviors associated with stress include marking, roaming, repetitive barking, destruction of property, and aggression. These are all ways in which dogs exteriorize inner tensions or stress.

In human athletes, stress is associated with an increased incidence of injury during athletic events. Presumably, the same principle applies to dogs. In addition, the endogenous steroids released in a stressed animal can cause delayed healing after injury. There are a number of medical conditions which can be worsened by stress. Stress increases the likelihood of heatstroke, can increase the frequency and/or severity of seizures, and can induce a variety of gastrointestinal problems including salivation, vomiting, and diarrhea.

Fig. 9.1. A relaxed and happy Golden Retriever in the conformation ring.

Fig. 9.2. One of the ways a water-loving dog can reduce stress.

REDUCING STRESS IN THE PERFORMANCE DOG

Stress cannot be totally prevented, but there are many things that can be done to ensure that a dog does not have exaggerated responses to environmental changes. Picking a puppy or adult with confidence in itself will go a long way towards preventing stress. A puppy should be exposed to as many experiences as

Table 9.1
Ways to Reduce Stress At Dog Shows

Make sure dog gets enough sleep
Bring dog bedding and toys from home
Do not feed too many new treats or food
Try not to share a hotel room
Do not leave dog alone in room for long periods
Train only briefly, if at all

possible while it is young. Guide Dogs for the Blind has determined that dogs that are brought up in a family and exposed to many new situations in their lives make better dog guides than those brought up in kennels. Dogs that are nervous when first exposed to new situations should be encouraged, not coddled. This will help them to be more bold and to investigate the unknown, rather than back off from the unfamiliar.

Human athletes suffering from staleness associated with longterm training or competition may have insomnia, decreased libido, decreased appetites, weight loss, and many of the signs of depression. Similar signs can be recognized in dogs that have been stressed by an intensive training or show schedule. Treatment involves rest, a reduced and varied training load, and play (Fig. 9.2).

Dogs should be kept at a correct and constant body weight and should be given regular exercise. Exercise causes the release of mood-elevating neurotransmitters in the brain. Be sure that your dog is kept on a regular schedule, especially during the performance season. Dogs thrive on routine, and a regular schedule of feeding and exercise can do much to relieve stress in a dog.

Because of the chance of serious infections, many people avoid bringing puppies to performance events until around four months of age, when their vaccinations are complete. This should, however, be balanced against the value of exposing the puppy to all the sights, sounds, and smells of dog shows and training venues during his formative first months. I take my 7-week-old puppies to performance events, but I am careful to let them play only in clean areas and with dogs that I know are fully vaccinated.

From the time a puppy attends its first performance event, every effort should be made to create a positive impression of these outings. This takes time

Fig. 9.3. Kermit and friend.

Fig. 9.4. The rewards of a long, enjoyable career.

and forethought. Puppies should be groomed and played with and talked to while at the show site. Frequently, in retrieving tests and other performance competitions, there is a break for lunch during which puppies can be walked around and familiarized with boats, decoys, sheep, and other tools of the trade.

Performance dogs should also be given some sort of routine, if possible, on show days. For example, the dog might be given a special toy which it associates with fun times (Fig. 9.3). Table 9.1 provides additional ideas for reducing stress at shows. Sometimes a dog will develop its own routine. One of my dogs, upon entering an obedience trial site, always jumps up and down at my side, barking with excitement. This behavior tells me he is not stressed. I scratch his back and tell him he's a good boy, let him bark five or six times and then tell him to be quiet. It's a routine that he chose and in which I participate. Stress-relieving games have helped him to enjoy competing well into old age (Fig. 9.4).

Probably the best, and most underused, prevention against stress is the use of play. Play with your dog when training, before and during competition, and in between time, just for fun. Play teaches dogs adaptive flexibility — the ability to accommodate to changes in their lives and environment.

Dogs differ individually in their responses to stress. When bringing multiple dogs to a performance event, it is easy to forget that one individual may need special attention to relax. It is important that you work on controlling your own nervousness and excitement and give quality time to each dog.

Most of all, before you begin the competition, talk quietly to your dog and tell him how great he is. Tell him (and mean it) that your relationship with him and the great stuff you do together during the rest of the week are so much more important that what happens in the next few minutes (Fig. 9.5). Because it's true.

Fig. 9.5. Tell him how great he is.

INDEX

swimming 121, 139, 175
sympathetic nervous system 32
synovial fluid 42

T

tail 26
    function 26
tarsal joint 33, 132. *See also* hock
tartar. *See also* calculus
teeth 17, 58, 79
temperament 61, 69, 100
temperament testing 70
tendons 41, 42
terriers 74, 179
tetracyclines 205
therapy 12
thyroid glands 31
thyroid hormone 207, 210
tibia 33
toes 35
tooth abscess 178
tooth cleaning 80
topline 26
Toy Poodle 14
trace metals 98
tracking 10, 17, 39, 61
trainability 57, 61
training
    duration of 115
    frequency of 115
    intensity of 115
tranquilizers 206
transcutaneous electrical nerve stimulation 129
transitional period 58
traumatic peripheral neuropathy 167
treadmills 121
triple pelvic osteotomy 148
trot 42, 48
trotting 39
turnspits 7

U

ulna 33
ultrasound 128, 129
undershot bite 16, 176
ununited anconeal process 151
upper respiratory tract infections 179
urinalysis 106

urinary System 30
urination
    increased 102

V

vaccinations 106
vegetables 99
vertebrae 24
veterinarian
    how to choose 103
    when to see 99
veterinary examination
    annual 104
visual acuity 20
vitamins 97
vocalization 28
volume of training 118
voluntary movement 40
vomiting 101
von Willebrand's Disease
    signs 192
    treatment 193
    and hypothyroidism 193

W

walk 42, 45
warm-up exercises 112
water
    daily intake 93, 125
weigh a dog
    how to 92
weight 89
weight change 92
weight loss
    technique for 92
Whippet 14, 26
whiskers 17
willingness to please 57
wobbler syndrome 155
wolves 6
wrist 33. *See also* carpal joint
wry mouth 176

Y

Yorkshire Terrier 23